CHANGING ETHNIC IDENTITIES

The Policy Studies Institute (PSI) is Britain's leading independent research organisation undertaking studies of economic, industrial and social policy, and the workings of political institutions.

PSI is a registered charity, run on a non-profit basis, and is not associated with any political party, pressure group or commercial interest.

PSI attaches great importance to covering a wide range of subject areas with its multi-disciplinary approach. The Institute's researchers are organised in groups which currently cover the following programmes:

Crime, Justice and Youth Studies – *Employment and Society* – *Ethnic Equality and Diversity* – *European Industrial Development* – *Family Finances* – *Information and Citizenship* – *Information and Cultural Studies* – *Social Care and Health Studies* – *Work, Benefits and Social Participation*

This publication arises from the Ethnic Equality and Diversity group and is one of over 30 publications made available by the Institute each year.

Information about the work of PSI, and a catalogue of available books can be obtained from:

Marketing Department, PSI
100 Park Village East, London NW1 3SR

1084333-7

Changing Ethnic Identities

Tariq Modood, Sharon Beishon and Satnam Virdee

POLICY STUDIES INSTITUTE
London

The publishing imprint of the independent
POLICY STUDIES INSTITUTE
100 Park Village East, London NW1 3SR
Telephone: 0171-387 2171   Fax: 0171-388 0914

ISBN 0 85374 646 X

PSI Research Report 794

A CIP catalogue record of this book is available from the British Library.

1 2 3 4 5 6 7 8 9

PSI publications are available from
BEBC Distribution Ltd
P O Box 1496, Poole, Dorset, BH12 3YD

Books will normally be despatched within 24 hours. Cheques should be made payable
to BEBC Distribution Ltd.

Credit card and telephone/fax orders may be placed on the following freephone
numbers:

FREEPHONE: 0800 262260
FREEFAX: 0800 262266

Booktrade representation (UK & Eire):
Broadcast Books
24 De Montfort Road, London SW16 1LW
Telephone: 0181-677 5129

PSI subscriptions are available from PSI's subscription agent
Carfax Publishing Company Ltd
P O Box 25, Abingdon, Oxford OX14 3UE

Laserset by Policy Studies Institute
Printed in Great Britain by Redwood Books, Trowbridge, Wilts.

Acknowledgements

This research was funded by the Joseph Rowntree Charitable Trust, to whom we are grateful. Nor would it have been possible without the participation of the interviewees. We would like to thank them and the Race Relations Committee of the London Borough of Waltham Forest, the Afro-Caribbean Elders Association of Waltham Forest, Jobs Through English Training (JET), Purehart Services, Plus Four and Anita Bedi for their support and help in finding the interviewees. Thanks are also due to Raj Raithatha and especially Shamsa Rana for their assistance as interviewers.

Within PSI the project was designed and initially supervised by David Smith and the writing up has benefited from the support and comments of Richard Berthoud, Head of Ethnic Equality and Diversity Group, Pam Meadows, Director, and Peter Willmott. We would also like to thank all those outside PSI who by commenting on an earlier draft helped us to improve this book, particularly Lisa Catan, Marian Fitzgerald, Dennis Brooks, Juliet Mountford, Bhikhu Parekh, David Gillborn and Gerhard Baumann. We are also grateful to Karin Erskine, Edwina Hodgson and Esther Lane for their invaluable assistance at the wordprocessor.

Contents

1 Introduction

In the post-war period, especially in the 1950s to the 1980s, there was considerable migration to Britain from some of the former colonies of the British Empire, in particular from the West Indies and the South Asian sub-continent. This came to mean that groups of people who had brought with them an ethnic identity distinct from the cultural patterns of what was sometimes referred to as the 'host' white community, became part of the population of Britain, especialy England. As groups and as individuals they were people who suffered from racial prejudice and discrimination, and found themselves excluded from many of the benefits and opportunities of British society. A large proportion of the research carried out over the 1960s, 1970s and 1980s, including PSI's own series of national surveys (Daniel, 1968, Smith 1977, Brown, 1984) was concerned with inequalities in their access to employment and housing, and with the direct and indirect discrimination associated with those inequalities.

Most of those who came to Britain as young men and women have reached or are reaching retirement, having spent all their adult life here. Many of their children were born here, and are now adults in their turn. Some have married white partners. While use of the term 'ethnic minority' has increased and is pervasive, it is no longer so obvious what an 'ethnic minority' consists of. The official census asks people to assign themselves to an ethnic group on the basis of a question combining colour and country/region of origin. This enables us to count how many people perceive themselves to be members of each group. However, whatever may have been the original meaning of 'ethnic minority', it is clear that the term is undergoing change as the people it describes are themselves changing and relating to the 'ethnic majority' in new ways.

Over the years the cultural patterns may have adapted in some way to the new environment. Members of the minority groups might have become more 'British'. Alternatively, their experience of discrimination, harassment and rejection might leave them feeling more isolated. The research reported here is concerned with some aspects of what it feels like to be a member of one of the main minority groups, and how it affects people's daily lives. It includes, for example, by what group label people like to be known, what they call themselves, what group they think they belong to and how it relates to other groups. It also includes questions about expressions of ethnic pride, styles of cultural adaptation and innovation, changes in patterns of family life and social contacts, extent of intra-community contact, attitudes to 'Britishness' and so on.

Unlike employment and housing, or even racial attacks and harassment, these topics have not yet featured in major surveys, so there is not an existing set of systematically connected data or even a set of standard questions against which one can measure change. Moreover, while there is a large body of research literature on some psychological aspects of identity – primarily on the alleged low self-esteem of black Americans, mainly children – the sociological and political aspects of contemporary ethnicity have not been investigated in a similarly systematic way. British studies of some sociological aspects of ethnic identity have been undertaken, but have been confined to just one or part of one ethnic group (eg Nevisians as in Byron, 1992) or, where more than one group is included, the study is confined to Asian groups (eg Stopes-Roe and Cochrane, 1990; Hutnik, 1991). Moreover, the samples are normally small and drawn only from one locality; these studies are often for a PhD and usually not published. Our ultimate aim is to research into at least some aspects of ethnic identity and cultural practices with a large sample and to make generalisations with a similar kind of scope and validity that one can make about, say, employment.

This book does not yet offer a quantitative map of ethnic minority identities. It offers a qualitative approach: relying not on numbers but the in-depth quality of respondents' thoughts and feelings, sensitively interpreted on the basis of a knowledge of respondents' cultural background, the pressures and tensions in their experiences, and a knowledge of the different strands and nuances in the debates about identitiy that are currently taking place. We do take one step forward from previous small-scale studies towards a more comprehensive understanding. We explore the issues of change and belonging with five different ethnic groups, not just different South Asian groups but also Caribbeans, within a single framework and explicitly compare and contrast the findings from each of these groups.

The research reported here is based primarily on detailed interviews or group discussions with 74 people, as described in more detail later in this Introduction. One of the outputs from the study has been the design of a structured set of questions about these issues to be included in PSI's fourth national survey of ethnic minorities, conducted jointly with Social and

Community Planning Research. That survey, based on interviews with 5,000 members of the main minority groups, will further extend our understanding of ethnic identity when the findings are published at the end of 1995.

Ethnic identities and 'race relations'
Before we set out the details about our study, we briefly explain why the topic studied here has become of growing importance and cannot be ignored by anyone interested in the shape, texture and dynamics of British race relations (Gilroy, 1987).

The reasons for the increase in consciousness and debate about ethnic identity in British society in general as well as among minority communities include the following.

New cultures
The time is long past when migration from the former Empire and Commonwealth to Britain could be understood in terms of the movement of labour, even though economic imperatives set it in motion. For out of that movement of labour have emerged, for at least some of the migrants, new communities capable of and perhaps wanting to maintain themselves as communities. With the ending of this period of movement, of uprooting and resettlement, it has become plain that new cultural practices, especially to do with the family and religion, have become a feature of the British social landscape, though it is far less clear which aspects may last for just one or two generations and which, if any, may be long term.

Public ethnicity
Minority ethnicity, albeit white ethnicity, has traditionally been regarded in Britain as acceptable if it was confined to the privacy of family and community, and did not make any political demands. Earlier groups of migrants and refugees, such as the Irish or the Jews in the nineteenth and the first half of the twentieth century, found that peace and prosperity came easier the less public one made one's minority practices or identity. Perhaps for non-European origin groups, whose physical appearance gave them a visibility that made them permanently vulnerable to racial discrimination, the model of a privatised group identity was never viable. Yet, additionally, one has to acknowledge the existence of a climate of opinion quite different from that experienced by the earlier Irish or Jewish incomers. In association with other socio-political movements such as feminism and gay rights which challenge the public-private distinction or demand a share of public space, ethnic difference is increasingly seen as something that needs not

3

just toleration but also public acknowledgement, resources and representation (Mendus, 1989; CRE, 1990; Young, 1990).

While political activism may have declined in some respects, for example in trade unions, there has been a burst of activism and discourse around minority issues and a demand for respect for minority groups. This new ethnic assertiveness has parallels with the United States, where ethnicity and race have traditionally had a higher social salience and political profile than in Britain, but it is less evident amongst recent migrants and their descendants in other European Union countries (Baldwin and Schwain, 1994). This assertiveness, based on feelings of not being respected or of lacking access to public space, often consists of counter-posing 'positive' images against traditional or dominant stereotypes, of projecting identities in order to challenge existing power relations or to negotiate the sharing of physical, institutional and discursive space. While there is not a comprehensive political consensus about the desirability of these public ethnicities, there is a vague multiculturalism as a policy ideology, which has perhaps contributed to the ethnic assertiveness. Certainly many of the race relations conflicts today (eg the Honeyford affair, the Rushdie affair, arguments about golliwogs, the Black and White Minstrels, 'political correctness') arise out of a demand for public space, for public respect and public resources for minority cultures and for the transmission of such cultures to the young.

Competition between identities

The non-white settlers, coming from several different parts of the world, brought with them a variety of nationalities, languages, religions, customs and loyalties. While some groups had no previous knowledge or contact with some of the others (say, Jamaicans and Punjabis) others who had experience of co-existence sometimes had historical antipathies and experience of intermittent conflict (say, Hindus and Muslims). The relation between Caribbeans and South Asians was further complicated by the fact that the former had known Indians in the Caribbean for over a century, whereas to the South Asian migrants to Britain the Caribbeans were strangers. There have been attempts to form a single 'black' constituency out of these settlers and their British-born descendants. Such attempts have sometimes seemed promising but have yet to succeed and it is not obvious that they will ever do so. Rather, the last few years have seen the emergence at a public level of a plurality of identities, of competition between identities and of the use of identities in the formation of pressure groups, coalitions and political solidarities to win public resources and representation and to influence policy-makers.

While some groups assert a racial identity based on the experience of having suffered racism, others choose to emphasise their family origins and homeland (even when they have never visited it or have no plans to do so), others group around a caste or a religious sect as do Hindus such as the Patels or Lohanas, while yet others promote a trans-ethnic identity like Islam. Yet the competition between identities is not simply a competition between groups: it is within communities and within individuals. It is quite possible for someone to be torn between the claims of being, for example, 'black', Asian, Pakistani and Muslim, of having to choose between them and the solidarities they represent or having to rank them, synthesise them or distribute them between different areas of one's life – and then possibly having to reconcile them with the claims of gender, class and Britishness.

Cultural-racism
While British racism has always consisted of a hostility directed at what are identified as inferior or primitive cultures, and while people from certain backgrounds have always been stereotyped in terms of alleged cultural traits, the cultural dimension has become more explicit. It could be argued that as a historical epoch compared to other historical periods of racism, for example nineteenth century biologism, the post-war period as a whole can be characterised as one of cultural-racism (Goldberg, 1993: 71). In any case, the presence of non-European origin cultural practices, the political claims made on their behalf and, by implication if not explicitly, the challenging of white British norms and symbols are giving rise to a counter-assertion in the form of new layers of racism and hostility. This cultural-racism is targeted at not just non-whites as such but at certain groups (groups perceived to be assertively 'different' and not trying to 'fit in'). Such racism uses cultural difference to vilify, marginalise or demand cultural assimilation from groups who also suffer colour-racism (Modood, 1994). Racial groups which have distinctive cultural identities or community life will suffer this additional dimension of discrimination and prejudice.

Reconceptualising race and ethnicity
Having to think about such issues is not simply to go beyond existing social survey instruments; it is tantamount to reconceptualising race relations. For the phenomena of which these four factors are part does not fit the American-derived conceptual and policy framework of 'race' and equality in which British thinking has been set (Modood, 1995). The underlying assumption of that framework is that the descendants of immigrants would lose all their 'difference' except colour and would therefore be thought of as a relatively undifferentiated 'black' mass both by themselves and by the

5

white British, and that the only area of conflict would be socio-economic – or more broadly of inclusion-exclusion into white British society.

Inclusion-exclusion is at the heart of the issue of ethnic minority identity but it is, as our fieldwork demonstrates, a far more complex matter than the simple American black-white approach. Developments in the United States – the emergence of black nationalism, Afrocentricism and the new multiculturalism based upon an increasingly varied population with large numbers of Hispanics and Pacific Asians – mean that today such an approach hardly has currency in the US. An alternative American social science approach, based upon studies of European immigrants as well as African-Americans, was partially eclipsed in the 1960s but is flourishing again as the nature and challenges of the plural character of American society come to the fore (Lal, 1990; Fuchs, 1990). These developments might even be seen as part of the waning of an Atlantocentic perspective, as peoples from outside the Atlantic area impinge upon it (Modood, 1995).

In any case the earlier influential American framework of 'race' is particularly inappropriate for Britain, where an important element is South Asian religious ethnicity, a feature absent from US black-white relations. While the new pluralistic American public discourse is about 'celebrating diversity', a sharp separation is made between ethnicity and religion; while the former is thought to be 'public', religion is thought to be 'private'. In Britain, however, it is not least the presence of Muslims (about half of all non-whites, and growing in both absolute and relative terms (Anwar, 1993)), exacerbated by their high international profile as the West's 'Other', that is changing British race relations and must be reflected in any attempt to take some measure of ethnic minority identities and culture (Modood, 1990, 1992 and 1994c). For this as well as for other reasons we thought it important to use the religions of the South Asian groups as one of the boundaries of ethnicity and to investigate the importance of religion and the relationship between religion and other components of ethnic minority identity.

While some of these identities are clearly of different kinds and have therefore the potential both to conflict with and be compatible with each other, they demonstrate that ethnic identities are not simply 'given' or fixed over time. The field of ethnic minority identities in Britain indeed displays the context-dependent and to some extent interest-dependent characters of identity. Yet these identities are not simply clothes hanging on a shop peg that can be tried on by the same person one after the other, or mixed and matched with varied accessories. There are historical continuities, living heritages, induction into customs and community norms, forms of socialisation within one's own community as well as through the state education system, the national media, youth culture, economic structures and racist practices – all of which can have an influence.

It is clear that these identities – what one calls oneself, to which community one thinks one belongs, which norms and sanctions are operative in one's life and to which minority causes and struggles one is willing to give time and energy – are open to adaptation and negotiation. They have also undergone, and are undergoing, change. In some cases this involves highlighting, even creating, distinctiveness and a sense of being apart. An even more powerful current is the movement from narrow identities to wider ethnicities or to extra-ethnic identities, to locating one's ethnic distinctiveness in a wider set of linked identities. This can be for a number of purposes including those of interest-group representation and political leverage, maximisation of individual freedom and choices, 'getting on', social harmony and patriotism. This development of broad or hyphenated identities is, of course, about how an ethnic group relates to other people, to other ethnic minorities and to the majority.

It may seem that the starting point of our study should be the pair of propositions that ethnic minority identities are a product of distinctive cultural practices, and that they are a product of how minorities believe they are treated by the majority. At one level this is indeed our starting point and the study is an inquiry into the interaction between these two propositions in practice. On the other hand, neither of these two propositions is quite true as it stands. Nimmi Hutnik, building upon the theories of Frederik Barth (Barth, 1969), has through a series of psychological experiments demonstrated that there is no simple link between minority cultural behaviour and minority ethnic identities (Hutnik, 1991). She found for example that of the young British Indians who said that they thought of themselves as Indians, many were not Indian in their cultural behaviour; conversely, some who were culturally Indian did not think of themselves as Indians (see also Stopes-Roe and Cochrane, 1990: 175). There is, that is to say, a genuine gap between self-definition and cultural practice. An ethnic identity, then, even that aspect of it which is based upon how the minority relates to the majority, cannot simply be read off from a description of distinctive cultures.

The proposition that locates minority identities in majority treatment of minorities is not quite true as it stands either. From the 1970s onwards many sociologists and others have argued that the defining condition of non-white people in Britain is racism; as racists represent all non-white people as 'black' this is the appropriate sociological description for all such groups and the natural public identity (eg CCCS, 1982; Haynes, 1983; Troyna, 1993; Keith, 1993). A crude but often used illustration of this point of view takes the following form: 'The skinhead who attacks you in the street does not distinguish between one kind of ethnic minority and another, so why should you?' We have to be careful, however, not to squeeze out the space for self-definition and think of minorities as just passive victims of racism. Minorities can identify their 'mode of oppression' without then going on to think of themselves as their oppressors see them. Some re-define themselves in terms of their oppression, but others may well have a more heightened sense of their 'mode of being' as a result of having to draw upon that aspect of their ethnicity which gives them the greatest self-pride and solidarity in the face of majority contempt (Modood, 1992). Just as strategies of ethnic self-categorisation have to be distinguished from the cultural content of an ethnicity, so strategies of self-definition, the symbolic and real forms of resistance against marginality, have to be distinguished between assertive strategies in terms of the mode of oppression and assertive strategies in terms of the victims' mode of being. Of course the two kinds of strategies can come together; the most successful example of which has been the marrying of the politics of anti-racism with a pride in African roots, creating a black political ethnicity, symbolised in the slogan 'black and proud'.

The focus of this study is only one kind of social identity, namely ethnic minority identity. Of course ethnic minority individuals, including those for whom an ethnic identity is of special importance, have several strands to their ethnic identity, but they also have numerous other identities based on occupation, neighbourhood, education, gender, hobbies and so on. Any one of these can be just as important to ethnic minority persons as an ethnic identity. This is perhaps a particularly important point as there is a growing body of evidence which suggests that ethnic minorities have now developed different socio-economic-educational profiles (Modood, 1992; Jones, 1993; Ballard and Kalra, 1994; Modood and Shiner, 1994). We do not here investigate ethnic identity within this broader sociological context. That is a task for the Fourth National Survey, through which, with its wide coverage of topics, we will be able to establish what correlations, if any, there are between certain forms of ethnic self-definition and, say, household size, type of neighbourhood, educational and employment experience, income level, political orientation, experience of discrimination and harassment. The present study aims to bring out, in the way that an omnibus quantitative survey by itself cannot, the diversity, ambivalences and complexities that currently characterise the changing nature of ethnic identities.

Table 1   Details of interviews

	Caribbeans	Pakistani Muslims	Bangladeshi Muslims	Punjabi Sikhs	Gujarati Hindus
Location	Walthamstow Birmingham	Walthamstow Birmingham	Whitechapel Birmingham	Gravesend Southall	Leicester Southall
Depth interviews	15	8	8	8	8
Group discussions	10	5	2	5	5
First generation	10	4	4	4	4
Second generation	15	9	6	9	9
Men	10	8	5	6	6
Women	15	5	5	7	7
Total	25	13	10	13	13

Research method and sample

The fieldwork consisted of exploring what ethnic identity meant to 74 people of Caribbean or South Asian origin through semi-structured interviews and group discussions. A breakdown of our sample is given in Table 1.

All five groups were studied in the Spring of 1993 in two locations where they formed a significant and settled population. This is an important point; all the people taking part lived in areas where other members of their group were well represented, and this is likely to have affected their perception of their group identity.

Personal interviews were carried out with eight members of each of the four Asian groups included in the study: four men and four women; four first generation and four second generation. The numbers were roughly doubled for the Caribbeans to ensure an adequate range of views among Caribbean respondents, for comparison with the Asian groups. The Caribbean, Pakistani and Bangladeshi interviewees were largely found through non-religious community organisations and through 'snowballing' using community activitist and friendship networks. The Punjabi and Gujarati interviewees were selected by knocking on people's doors in the designated area and recruiting participants until the desired number of each generation and gender was reached.

The interviews were conducted by researchers who were members of, and spoke the languages of, the minority communities. Some repsondents,

9

mostly from among the first generation Punjabi and Gujarati migrants, were interviewed in the language of origin. The interviews lasted an hour, sometimes more. The interviews with Caribbeans, Pakistani and Bangladeshi respondents were tape-recorded. Notes were made by the interviewer during the interviews with Gujaratis and Punjabis.

Three group discussions were held, one with Caribbeans, one with a mixed group of Gujaratis and Punjabis and the third with a mixed group of Pakistanis and Bangladeshis (the last discussion group included two mixed-ethnicity persons). The two Asian groups were confined to second generation individuals in order to reflect the comparative youthfulness of that population and to enhance the focus on changes and new currents. Participants were recruited by a market research agency and were paid a small fee for their participation. They were led by a researcher who was a member of (one of) the ethnic groups under consideration. They lasted about an hour and a half, and were tape-recorded.

About three-quarters of the contact time was taken up with questions or discussions about ethnic identity, cultural background, social contacts and the related matters which are presented in this book; the remainder of the time was spent on health, giving and receiving care and racial harassment (the findings on the last topic are published in a separate report (Virdee, 1995)).

The size of our sample and the methods by which it was selected mean that it is not necessarily representative of the respective population groups. For a detailed discussion of the frequency of various views or practices in different communities and their correlations with socio-economic factors, we have to await the findings of the National Survey. The interest of the present study lies in identifying the range of views held and seeing how they are articulated and elaborated by those who hold them. While on a purely numerical basis this study cannot compete with the National Survey, with its sample of about 5,000, it is widely recognised that semi-structured interviews and discussions allow people to speak for themselves in a way not possible with a structured questionnaire (Hammersley and Atkinson, 1983; Burgess, 1984). This study thus provides qualitative material which allows us to examine the texture of opinion. The willingness to give up some of their time and to subject themselves to sensitive questions may itself make our respondents unrepresentative and, particularly with the Caribbeans, Pakistanis and Bangladeshis, our sample may well be biased towards those relatively active in their ethnic communities or in activity such as lobbying for public services or funds. They may therefore have a stronger or different sense of ethnic identity from ethnic minority individuals generally; it is just as likely that they give expression to ideas which are in the process of becoming more influential in their communities. Either way, the purpose of the study will be achieved if it is gives some insight into the minority debates that are taking place and shaping the nature of British race relations.

Some methodological issues

Some more needs, however, to be said about our structuring of the sample, about who we chose and who we excluded. In the 1991 Census, three million people or 5.5 per cent of the population categorised themselves (or were categorised by the adult member of the household filling in the census form) as belonging to an ethnic group other than white. About half of this population were categorised by a South Asian national identity (Indian, Pakistani, Bangladeshi) and nearly a quarter by black-Caribbean and black-Other (most of the latter were British-born people with Caribbean origins). It is on these two sets of groups that we have focused.

As the Indian group (which includes East African Asian) is the largest of all these groups and includes several quite distinct strands, we sub-divided it into Punjabis and Gujaratis (many but not all of which have an East African connection). As nearly all Pakistanis and Bangladeshis are Muslims, to ensure that we had sufficient numbers of Hindus and Sikhs in our sample, we included no Indian Muslims. We wanted to explore the influence of religion in the various South Asian identities, but the sizes of our samples did not allow us to include minority South Asian religions such as Christianity or Zoroastrianism. Nor, for the same reason, were we able to explore the cases when the major religions were a minority within an ethnic group, for example, Hinduism within British Punjabis. We therefore confined our attention to the major religion within each South Asian group, thus creating the following four distinct ethno-religious groups:

- Pakistani Muslims

- Bangladeshi Muslims

- Punjabi Sikhs

- Gujarati Hindus

The groups created are slightly artificial but not as much as they might seem, for religion here simply refers to a family religious affiliation, to the religion one was born into, and not to an individual's profession of faith, let alone practice. We are using religion as an element of ethnicity, and nearly everyone in each national or regional group is in fact affiliated to the religious community we have singled out. While socio-economic studies tend to use national origins to sub-divide South Asians (some studies, for

11

example, Drew et al, 1992, present Asians as a homogeneous group), and cultural studies tend to use religion (eg Stopes-Roe and Cochrane, 1990), we have chosen to combine the two forms so as to be able to explore the relationship between them in relation to issues of culture and identity.

With the Caribbeans too a double criteria was used to select respondents. In their case a Caribean origin was supplemented with an African ancestry. Our respondents do not therefore include any of the other groups, such as Indians, who are present, albeit in small numbers, amongst the West Indian population. Strictly speaking, therefore, this group ought to be called Black-Caribbean, African-Caribbean or Afro-Caribbean. For the sake of brevity and because neither the people themselves nor commentators are at the moment agreed on which of these hyphenated terms is most appropriate, we have decided to simply use the term 'Caribbean'.

A central interest of the study was generational differences or, more precisely, the effects of a British upbringing and socialisation. Our sample, consisting of 49 South Asians and 25 Caribbeans, with roughly equal proportions of women and men, was not evenly spread across the age-bands but clustered around the ages of 60 and 20. People were chosen because they were adult migrants or because they were born in and/or brought up in Britain. The formal criteria we used to create these two bands were:

- People from our selected ethnic groups who were born in and received their schooling or worked until the age of 16 or over in the country from which they migrated.

- People from our selected ethnic groups who were born in and received their schooling in Britain, or if not born in Britain, received their schooling in Britain.

The criteria were not based on age as such but on where the formative years (up to the age of 16) were spent. In practice this amounted to a generational difference and we call the migrants 'the first generation' and the British-born 'the second generation'. These are far from satisfactory terms; as has just been explained, they do not strictly speaking refer to generations at all. Hence the youngest of our first generation sample, a Gujarati man of age 29, is younger than a couple of our second generation sample. Nevertheless, most of the first generation group are in their sixties, with most of the rest being in their fifties; and nearly all of the second generation are in their late teens and twenties.

There are, however, further problems specifically with the term 'second generation'. One of these is that our sample consists mainly of what could be described as the third rather than the second generation; the method by which we constructed our sample omits those who came to Britain as older children and therefore whose upbringing and schooling spans the country of their birth and Britain (sometimes referred to as 'the half-way generation') and who would perhaps cluster around the age of 40. Certainly the relation between our two samples is much more like that of grandparents and grandchildren, rather than of parents and children, but we thought that the reader would find it strange to be constantly reading of a 'first' and a 'third' generation without any reference to a 'second'.

We do not mean 'second generation' to be shorthand for 'second generation immigrant' for of course they are not immigrants at all; 'second generation' is here short for 'adult second generation Gujaratis (or another ethnic group)'. Despite the awkwardness of the term we thought it better than, say, 'British Gujaratis', with its instant suggestion that the first generation were not British, and marginally better than, say, 'the British-born generation' (which we could use for, as it turned out, all of our second generation sample were born in Britain). No terminology, it seems to us, is going to be without its infelicities. The terminology we are using reflects our interest in *change* and reflects also our view that the period of living in Britain, in particular of growing up in Britain, is an important factor in understanding the changes that have been and are taking place.

It is important to note also that the ethnic minority population groups differ in terms of period of residence in Britain and in their age structures. The Caribbeans are the longest established, with nearly all of the migrants coming here in the 1950s and 1960s (Jones, 1993: 25). While much of the male South Asian migration too took place in the same period, family reunification, the arrival of wives and children, tended to begin only towards the end of this period, the process completing itself in the 1970s for Indians, 1980s for Pakistanis, and is perhaps even yet not completed for Bangladeshis. Asian refugees from East Africa, who form about a third of the Indian immigrants (Ballard and Kalra, 1994: 6), unlike migrant workers from the sub-continent, tended to come to Britain as families, though they too came mainly in the 1970s. For these reasons, as well as differential rates of fertility, the Asian population in general and the Pakistanis and Bangladeshis in particular are much younger than the white population, while the Caribbean age structure is roughly similar to that of whites (Ballard and Kalra, 1994).

Both these features, the differential period of settlement and the age structure, were reflected in our sample. While the first generation Caribbeans and Punjabis had been in Britain between 30 and 40 years, the period was less for the other Asians, usually over 20 years, though sometimes under ten years, as was the case with three Gujaratis. Similarly,

13

in both generations the Punjabis and Caribbeans tended to be a bit older than the others.

It perhaps goes without saying that it is in the nature of the subject, ethnic identity, as well as of the methods used, that there are no simple 'objective' findings. Nearly everything depends on the interview: the rapport and relationship established between the interviewer and interviewee, the nature and degree of probing, the time given to a particular topic, even the tone of voice and facial expression with which a question may be asked. Moreover, it is critical that the two (or more) parties are using a common vocabulary and understand its nuances and implications. And interpretation is critical at all levels: the interpretation of the question by the interviewee; the interpretation of an answer by the interviewer (which determines what other questions are and are not asked, what avenues are explored); the interpretation the researcher puts on the tape recording or their notes when it comes to selecting, ordering and writing up the material; and, finally, the theoretical interpretation or commentary put upon the findings.

The process is even more complicated with group discussions where some participants can have undue influence and where not all can contribute to every single item of discussion. Where there can be no 'neutrality' we cannot apologise for its absence. So far as we have 'a line' it is that the ethnic minority situation is more complex, more plural than many researchers and spokespeople suggest. We have wanted to give our respondents an opportunity to have their diverse voices heard. To this end we employed interviewers who were themselves members of the relevant ethnic groups in the belief that this would encourage a more open response and a more ready understanding. A feature of this project is that all the different stages of interpretation mentioned above have been undertaken by minority ethnic individuals.

The following chapters typically have a tripartite structure: there is a report on the views of the Caribbeans, followed by a report on the South Asians, followed by some interpretative comments. We recognise that the findings could have been structured in other ways. For example, we initially planned to write a report on a group by group basis. We found, however, that the similarities between the different South Asian groups entailed considerable repetition. Yet to combine all five groups, including the Caribbeans, into a single account was difficult to do. Again, a sharp separation between report and commentary, while not uncommon, is perhaps taken further here than in some other ethnographic studies. It was felt that this form allowed us to reserve comment, which is often comparative in nature, until the relevant views of all the groups had been reported. It also gave us the freedom to comment just on those matters where we thought the commentary added something to the material, and it allowed us to range widely in the discussion while leaving the reader free to interpret the views of the respondents themselves.

Finally, a further word on nomenclature. We recognise that there is barely any terminology, whether about the groups as a whole ('ethnic minorities', 'non-whites', 'blacks') or about a specific group (for example should it be 'Afro-Caribbean', 'African-Caribbean', 'black' or 'black British'? should Pakistanis be referred to as Muslims?) which is uncontested. Since the issue of labels and their contestation is part of the subject of our inquiry and since, as will be seen later, respondents themselves held different views, often passionately, we have tried to use what we believe are descriptive terms that leave the debates relatively open rather than close them.

2 Family and Social Contacts

The family is an important component of ethnicity. It is where individuals start life and first acquire a conception of self and of others. The nature of their upbringing and family life may be different from or be perceived as being different from that of others. Families may transmit a culture and may be the main link people have with what they perceive as their ethnic group. If family structures have changed or are changing this may mean significant changes in ethnicity in terms of the transmission of heritages, contact with and forms of obligations to members of one's ethnic group; and conversely, in terms of contact and relationships with people outside one's family and group. Similarly, the character of changes or the absence of changes may contribute to or weaken a sense of being culturally different from the rest of the population, of being British.

We sought to find out what family life meant for our respondents, in what ways, if any, it was important to them, whether and how it contributed to a sense of ethnic identity, and how the experiences of the migrants and the British-born varied. We also asked our respondents about the contexts in which friendships were formed, and about the ethnic background of their friends, to see what extent ethnic identity was relevant to choice of friends. We were also interested in whether they had other kinds of social contact, for example, working for or receiving assistance from a voluntary organisation, where ethnicity was relevant or which made respondents think about obligations to members of their ethnic group.

Caribbeans
All the Caribbean respondents felt it was important to keep in contact with family members. A number of reasons were given to do with the emotional and material support given and received within the family. Shared experiences within the family led to a feeling of mutual understanding and closeness. As one respondent said: 'We have got that bond between us.' One respondent spoke of a 'physical need' to be in contact with the family. Others described the family as 'a part of you' and of 'being lost' without it. Respondents felt feelings of duty and responsibility towards family

members. In particular parents were singled out for special praise and respect. Giving support to family members was considered to be one of the most important functions a family carries out. 'We should help others, but family must come first.'

For Caribbean families this often took on extra meaning. Families were part of the coping strategy used by individual members to deal with racism and discrimination on a daily basis.

As a black family it is even more important to give support because of the extra problems we face.

In both generations there was a very strong sense of how the Caribbean family had been transformed. This was partly because of having moved away from small, often rural, communities.

Our village was small, everyone was family. It was not as if my mum had to ask someone to look after the children. If a parent was not there, there was automatically another [quasi] parent.

Back 'home' there was a community that actively helped and supported others. Respondents, both first and second generation, spoke of a notion of the family as they believed it had once operated in the Caribbean. For some, an informal welfare system functioned within the family and wider community, including those friends overseas who sent money and goods 'home'. Another example was the way in which children were considered the responsibility of the whole community, with children from families in need being informally adopted.

The extended family was a great source of help. But now it's not allowed to help in the same way as before. For instance, relatives cannot take a child, [to look after and bring up if the parents are in difficulties] because of the law. The African compound which we lived in physically and mentally has broken up.

It was not only that the extended family no longer exists in the same way as before. There is also a recognition that the obligations and motivations between family members have changed. As one parent put it:

You should not have to go to strangers when you have your own children, you should be able to depend on them first... I would want to say it's their duty, but everyone has got their own life to lead and their own mind.

In general Caribbean parents felt that their children were very British in outlook and attitude: 'they look at things differently than I do'. For this mother, the contrast with the past centred on her children regularly questioning situations and assumptions. Children often ignored what they were told by parents and gave their own interpretations. This mother felt it would have been unacceptable for her to behave in this way with her own parents. It would not have been considered acceptable to question parents, regardless of your age.

First generation mothers suggested,however,that there had been a change not only in how their children behaved with them, but in how they 'parented' their children. They had developed new types of relationship. First generation parents felt that the relationship they now have with their children is a more equal one. Parents and grown-up children interact as 'friends', with advice and support flowing in both directions.

There are a lot of things I accept that my parents would not accept; like my children telling me exactly what they think, their opinion... Children are not afraid to tell you what they think and live their life how they see best.

There are now few areas that are off limits in discussions with children. Respect was no longer automatically given by children to all adults, elders or parents. Some parents found this change difficult to understand. They spoke of the 'back-home' attitude and the differences in the ways in which they interact with their parents.

Respecting your parents, which is something we do back home. Bringing up your children a certain way, to respect you and others. I still have that way towards my mother and step-father.

Parents felt that obedience to parents was no longer practised by younger generations. As one parent put it: 'They will take advice from you, but that does not mean they will do it.' Most second generation women described their mothers as taking a traditional role within the family unit. Mothers were primarily responsible for the home and family regardless of whether they were in paid employment as well. The home and family was seen as the focus of their mothers' lives. Opportunities for their mothers outside of this were considered to be limited. Second generation women suggested not only that they are more ambitious, but they have access to wider and more varied opportunities.

The changed nature of the family and relationships within it was evidenced by the fact that only half the Caribbean respondents had regular or frequent contact with their extended family outside the circle of parents, children and siblings. Uncles, aunts, cousins and other wider family members were rarely seen on a regular or frequent basis. This was not just a generational difference. Many felt the process of migration had broken up the wider family network. Often it was only the younger adult members of a family who had migrated,and not just to Britain, but also to USA and

Canada, producing an even wider dispersion. Even in Britain families were not always living near one another, and it was certainly the exception rather than the rule that extended families shared the same residence. As families established themselves and had families themselves, contact had inevitably decreased, partly off-set by the use of the telephone and letters. Location was, however, the key factor for families resident in the same country, regular contact being often dependent upon living locally.

Only two second generation respondents felt that levels of contact within the family had been maintained. One respondent related how his family had tried to recreate a structure similar to that in the Caribbean. All family members who had migrated to the UK had settled in a single location and lived within streets of one another. This had led to a 'back-home atmosphere' and a 'bondness' between family members which had been instilled in them as children. This in turn had enabled them to continue the family tradition themselves. With most respondents there was a general feeling that once people had families of their own they would drift away from their original family unit. Priorities changed within the life-cycle of the family. These changes have in fact also taken place within the Caribbean itself and are a product of urbanisation as well as migration.

One of the ways in which members of a family help each other is financially. Changes in attitudes and practice in this respect are therefore a useful measure of change in family structures. Almost all of the first generation respondents would expect financial help from their partners, siblings or children if they needed it. These respondents felt that immediate family members had an obligation to help financially if required. However, none of these parents expected their children to contribute financially as a matter of course. All of the first generation displayed strong feelings of monetary independence. Nevertheless, if a situation arose and money was needed respondents felt that children and partners should and could be relied upon. Only a few considered finance to be a personal matter on which each individual must be responsible for him or herself.

Only four respondents (from both first and second generations) expected the wider family to give financial help when needed. In fact more respondents suggested that close friends rather than wider family members would be looked to for financial help. All second generation respondents suggested they would turn to family members only for fairly small amounts needed in the short term for domestic or daily items. Second generation respondents were less likely to expect help from family members and more likely to turn to financial institutions such as banks and building societies. Two second generation respondents felt that no one had a duty to help them even in dire financial circumstances. Four had a sense of financial self-reliance similar to that among first general respondents.

A half-way house between borrowing from family and friends and from a bank is the 'Pardner' system for saving and borrowing money.It was recognised by all respondents,including those who had not used it. It is based on a Yoruba system of saving and loaning money. A group of people regularly deposit sums of money over a fixed interval with a principal individual, the 'banker', in a central fund. Each person in the group takes a turn in withdrawing their 'hand' which is usually the total amount collected for that week or month. The scheme operates completely on trust as there is usually no written agreement. As such, it tends to operate amongst friends, families or close groups of other kinds. Its advantages are that no interest is charged and there are no forms to be filled out or bureaucracy to work through. Relatively large sums of money can be saved and obtained when it is one's turn to draw out. The system is widely used by African-Caribbean communities in all parts of the globe (Senior 1991).

Four first generation respondents had used this system in the past. All first generation respondents spoke of the difficulties of borrowing money for home purchase from financial institutions in the 1950s and 1960s. Two of these originally used the Pardner scheme to raise funds for home deposits and at least one first generation respondent was still participating in one. It is now more frequently used for saving for smaller purchases, usually in conjunction with other more formal borrowing or savings schemes.

Two second generation respondents were currently involved in a Pardner. For one, money raised in this way would contribute towards the purchase of a home. Other second generation respondents were more likely to ask friends or family for financial help and were less reserved about approaching banks and building societies.

Beyond the family, the church provided one of the primary networks from which first generation respondents made and sustained friendships. Five first generation respondents mentioned the church or church-related activities as the arena in which they had first made acquaintances with those whom they now considered friends. Work as a site of association was less common. This may be a reflection of retirement, for most first generation respondents were retired. There was little difference in the types of activity engaged in amongst friends and amongst families. Social activities ranged from visiting each others' homes, going to the theatre, cinema and local community organisations to going on holiday together. Going to church, church related events and religious activities such as reading the Bible, singing hymns and theological debates were favoured by over half of this group.

Most first generation respondents had friendship circles that encompassed peoples of varied nationalities and ethnicities. At least one respondent felt that having a wide range of friends brought explicit advantages. The learning and exchanging of different languages and cultures led to a broadening of horizons and had expanded his outlook on the world and its peoples. When it came to close friends, half of first generation respondents had only Caribbean close friends. None suggested this was a conscious decision, although the sentiments of one suggested otherwise: 'I don't believe that white friends can be genuine. They really just want to take advantage.'

This respondent felt that in a crisis some of her white friends would not 'put themselves out' to help. None of these five respondents felt there were any disadvantages in having close friends exclusively from one ethnic group, though they did not think that it was a requirement either. One respondent felt that shared origins brought certain advantages.

There are certain things you can talk about. Growing up in St. Lucia, which is similar to how you grew up in Dominica, you can relate. Personally, I don't think I can relate to a white person. I can tell them, but it won't be the same as talking to my friends from St. Lucia, from Grenada, from Jamaica.

For her, growing up in the Caribbean laid the foundations of commonality which was still operative in 'relating' to others as close friends.

Second generation respondents mentioned a wider sphere in which to meet and make friends. Of primary importance were school, college and work. Two respondents suggested the influence of the family in making friends. Those who were actively involved within their own families were less likely to have friends outside of this network. Many friends were also members of their own family.

About two-thirds of the British-born respondents had friends of various nationalities and ethnicities. Friendships were largely based on similar interests, shared experiences and location. A friend was seen frequently and therefore needed to live, work or socialise in the respondent's vicinity. For this, group ethnicity was not of direct importance in choosing friends but entered indirectly. The focus was on shared activities or shared interests, for example, certain types of music or club. These activities were usually mixed-ethnicity but often within Caribbean or African-American inspired cultural styles. This was often explained as white friends being brought up in 'black culture' because of the multi-racial area in which they lived.

Most of the other second generation respondents whose friendships were predominantly with other black people did not explicitly suggest that this was a policy operated on their part but that their friendships too were framed around shared experiences, activities and localities. Even when respondents were asked to distinguish between friends and close friends, only six said that they had close relationships exclusively with other black people. Three only, however, actually felt there were particular advantages in having one's close friends all from one's own ethnic group. There was a feeling of being 'at ease' as well as a greater depth of understanding: 'I can relate to the struggles they have had'.

The struggles were often against discriminatory and racist practices. Other black friends were thought able to offer a deeper level of support precisely because they themselves had gone through similar experiences. These respondents felt there was an 'extra bond' and a level of understanding beyond that offered by white friends. For two respondents there was the added issue of intimacy and a reluctance to 'open up' to someone who did not reflect them emotionally and psychologically. Two respondents, however, suggested that having friends exclusively from a single ethnic group would, if they were not careful, lead to them becoming intransigent and fixed in their outlook.

Beyond family and friendships we were also interested to what extent there was a sense of belonging to a community, more particularly the sense of active participation in community activities, and whether that participation was influenced by ethnic group considerations. The method of recruitment of respondents to this project meant the level of activity in community organisations was high. Thirteen respondents were actively involved in community organisations and activities. Seven of these were first generation respondents who were active as either beneficiary or organiser of a local Afro-Caribbean organisation. For the other six, involvement had evolved out of contacts made through their work or through friends or relatives already active in such groups. Most of these organisations and activities were specific to Caribbean women or elders or were fund raising activities for black charities. The majority of these respondents voluntarily gave their time and skills to support less able members of the community. Activities ranged from management activities and fundraising to informal help and support on a daily basis.

Yet even in a group so active in community work, only one first generation respondent explicitly mentioned the ethnicity of the group as important, as wanting to help 'my people'. What was of most importance for the others was being accepted and feeling comfortable with other members of the voluntary group, regardless of ethnicity. Three of the six second generation respondents involved in community activities had in fact made a conscious decision to become involved in community groups specifically aimed at other African-Caribbeans.

Two major themes were apparent. First, a feeling of being comfortable and enjoying the presence of other Caribbeans. There was a feeling of affinity which arose from being able to identify with other Caribbeans. Secondly, there was a feeling of exclusion from non-ethnic specific community groups. As one respondent put it: 'Most organisations only cater for the white majority'.

There was a feeling of invisibility and under representation in multi-ethnic community groups. Older Caribbeans said they were not comfortable in environments that did not cater for their needs, especially in terms of food and language. One respondent described the cultural isolation by imagining the situation in reverse.

If we were to start to introduce English people into the group and we start speaking our language, they won't understand what we are talking about, so they won't fit in at all. They would feel lost.

Both first and second generation respondents spoke of the isolation felt by black elders in multi-ethnic support groups that were unwilling or unable to provide a level of sensitivity. There was a high level of concern over state provision and local government facilities for Caribbeans. It was felt therefore that Caribbeans had a special responsibility to help each other; a sense of collective welfare arising out of the failure of the mainstream structures (see also Jayaweera, 1993).

One respondent showed how this sense of ethnic welfare could emerge. He had not made a conscious decision to take part in an ethnic-specific group but, because of the composition of the local community, he found himself leading a group of predominantly Caribbean children. Wanting to give them self-confidence, he made a decision to develop a cultural dimension in his voluntary work. In his view it was important for the children to learn something about black history and culture, which was absent from their schooling, so as to 'get in touch with their roots'. It was their cultural deprivation in the school system that made ethnicity important in his voluntary work. Some first and second generation respondents went further. For them the purpose of activity within such ethnic specific groups was not to find a safe and comfortable environment or even collective welfare, but rather to promote a sense of unity within the black community, a unity that could be achieved in part by the community taking care of its own wherever possible.

On the other hand, two respondents had a preference for multi-ethnic community groups and organisations. For these two, there was a belief that meeting and sharing with people from other backgrounds and ethnicities would bring communities closer together. Over time this process would lead to greater tolerance and a decline in overall prejudice. These respondents felt that this could be achieved only in mixed ethnicity groups.

South Asians

On these as on other topics studied in this book, we found among South Asians a marked difference between the first and second generations, and so our presentation takes this generational form.

First generation respondents felt it was extremely important to be in contact with the family. This meant being in contact not only with their own immediate family but also with the extended family comprising grandparents, uncles, aunts, cousins, and their spouses, in-laws and children. For such respondents the extended family system was the central institution through which mutual support to each member of the family was given. In addition, it was here that particular codes of behaviour based on religious and cultural values were passed on to members of the younger generation.

First generation people explained that they were brought up with a strong sense of duty to the extended family. This entailed a large portion of one's life being centred around the activities of the extended family.

> *I believe in keeping strong ties within the family. We meet each other every two or three days. We shop together, go out together. Sleep over at each other's house. We share almost every aspect of our lives together.*

All the first generation respondents had members of their extended family living locally and saw them once or twice a week. This contact would take place mainly in each other's houses or at social and religious functions at places of worship. A first generation woman explained the importance of this level of activity as:

> *In order to reinforce feelings of close relationships with the whole family and to ensure that my daughters have knowledge of the exact relationship to each relative and have gained it through contact.*

A result, as another interviewee noted, was that people always had someone to turn to for company and comfort, for there was: 'always someone around with whom you can talk'. Indeed, one of the benefits of a closely-knit family system was that senior family members took an active interest in everyone's well-being: 'the elders recognise if there are difficulties in a marriage and will help to straighten it out before it becomes a problem'.

It was noticeable that the Pakistanis and Bangladeshis had a high level of contact with family in their countries of origin. The majority of first generation respondents from these groups visited the country in question at least every other year and letters were written weekly and phone calls made monthly to relatives. Several first generation migrants, especially Bangladeshis, financially assisted their family abroad, for example in helping to meet the costs of schooling nephews and nieces, recognising that living in Britain allowed them to be better off than many of their relatives.

As a result of this strong commitment to the extended family, the first generation spent little leisure time outside this circle. The friends they had outside the family tended to be members of their ethnic group whom they had known since the time of migration or earlier. Socialising consisted of going round to each other's houses for dinner and a chat. Most of the first generation were not involved in any organisations except the local temple or mosque, though some were active in voluntary community relations work. Most had no friends from outside their community. Work acquaintances were mentioned but were not included among social contacts.

Some respondents mentioned the limitations of language in explaining why their friends were of their own ethnic group. One Sikh first generation woman also mentioned the importance of a common faith and how it made it possible to share and talk through problems from a taken-for-granted point of view. Muslim respondents, too, emphasised the importance of close friendships being based upon shared 'values and attitudes towards life'. This was regarded as extremely important because Muslim friends understood the 'restrictions in your life and there was no tension of having to go to a party or event where there was alcohol or any other non-Islamic practices'. Respondents did not express opposition to the idea of friendships across ethnic or religious lines but recognised that the circumstances of their lives, including the sometimes stressful experience of migration and early settlement in Britain, worked against friendships across racial and ethnic lines. A Muslim migrant felt excluded from some of the ways that relationships at work developed:

> They expect you to interact with them at a social level, which is normally in the pub. But being a Pakistani and a Muslim, I don't drink. If I do go to the pub and drink an orange juice people try to make me feel bad because I'm not drinking alcohol. They try to say that I am doing something wrong by not drinking alcohol.

First generation women were even less likely to have close friendships outside their ethno-religious group. They were more likely to have or to have had difficulties in speaking English and more likely to work mainly with members of their own group and have little or no social life outside the family. Where they were involved in local organisations, as were two Gujarati women with a temple and a Pakistani woman with an Urdu class for children, it was explicitly for members of their own group. Where their circle of friends went beyond their ethnic or religious group, it usually consisted of Asians, as with a Pakistani woman who knew quite well up to ten Indian families, only some of whom were Muslim.

The second generation respondents' patterns of contact were, on the whole, markedly different from those of the first generation. Most were like their parents in the importance they attached to contact with the immediate family. This was partly because of a sense of duty to the family and also of an appreciation of the importance of an institution which offered 'reassurance, stability and support'.

> *The support I have got up to the age I am now is terrific. I couldn't get that anywhere else. This support goes on through your whole life. For example, when you have your first baby, your mother will be there. That is very important.*

The specialness of family relationships was referred to consistently during the interviews.

> *Friends and colleagues are one thing but contact with family is important in terms of knowing who you are. It is important, a 'must', to keep in touch with your family.*

There was also a recognition amongst the second generation that it was within the confines of the immediate family, in particular, that people would learn how to behave in the wider society. The family as a social institution would be responsible for instilling morals and ethics into a particular individual, which, in turn, would influence how he or she would behave in the wider society.

> *It is only within the family that you can learn about sharing, being generous, unselfish and helping others.*

Or, as another second generation interviewee explained, contact with the family made one aware that:

> *... apart from yourself there are others who have problems. It helps you to realise you are not the only one who has problems. Contact fosters the right kinds of values and it is important to put yourself second.*

Most of the British-born generation, because of their age, had limited experience in financial and property transactions and, therefore, in extended family matters of that kind. But it was noticeable that the Bangladeshis and

Pakistanis were in closer touch with extended family members in Britain and their country of origin than the Indians, and that each of the Bangladeshis who had worked had given financial assistance to members of the extended family. (One respondent spoke of how straight after the interview he was joining a gathering of family members at a relative's house in London to grieve and pray following a drowning of a cousin in Bangladesh.)

This commitment to the family was reflected in the level of contact the second generation had with their parents and grandparents. If the second generation respondents were not living with their parents or grandparents, they saw them on average once every two weeks. This commitment to the immediate family was not, however, translated into a strong commitment to the extended family. On average, the second generation saw their uncles and aunts only once every two or three months at social gatherings such as weddings and birthdays.

It is clear that a significant generational change has taken place in the pattern of social contacts. The result of being brought up and educated in Britain was a social life centred less on the extended family and ethnic community and more on activities connected with work or educational institution. Consequently, the patterns of contact tended to be more diffuse and diverse than those of the first generation. This could be seen with the second generation respondents who were or had been students in the recent past. Some Indians highlighted their involvement in a number of student societies not related to their ethnic group, including a History Society and a Wine Society, as well as writing for the college newspaper. This had brought them into contact with people from other ethnic groups and had enabled them to develop close friendships with some of them. Moreover, they felt their social interests, such as going to nightclubs, theatres and cafes, were similar to those of most other students at university. However, these students maintained a number of close Asian friends and retained some link with their ethnic group through their involvement in the university Punjabi Society and the Hindu/Sikh Cultural Society.

Similarly, those second generation members currently in employment also explained that, because they had gone through the education system with other ethnic groups, they had friends from other ethnic groups, and that this caused no problems. Nearly all were involved in activities in and outside work that led to the formation of friendships across ethnic groups. One woman was a trades union steward who represented her workforce in negotiations with management. Two second generation individuals were now in the process of establishing a local youth centre for children from all ethnic groups in their local area.

One Gujarati respondent said that she and her husband were professionals who were both heavily involved in social activities concerning their work. As a result, she said, a large proportion of their friends were white. Although she still attended social and religious gatherings at the local place of worship, she felt she was far less involved with them than were her parents, her mother in particular. One of the two mixed-ethnicity Asians said that she felt much more accepted by white people because culturally she related to them much better and consequently she had mainly white friends; the other mixed-ethnicity Asian said that he mixed with everyone who enjoyed the things he enjoyed, such as clubbing. A Bangladeshi man, in contrasting his life with that of his father, summed up the situation for many of his generation.

My Dad now, his life was working from seven in the morning to eight at night. All he did was eat, work, go to bed, day after day, try to save as much as you can to go back or send back to his family. They didn't integrate with the community, didn't want to, probably didn't know how to. My life is completely different, educated here, have black, white, Asian friends, I socialise, go out to discos...

Most second generation respondents thought that going through the education system had allowed them a greater degree of close contact with people from different ethnic groups than their parents had had. As a result the centre of their social lives was not the extended family and the ethnic community but rather friends who simply shared similar related interests, especially ones related to education.

Nevertheless, for most British-born Asians, their closest friends were from their own ethnic background or, at least, Asian. Sometimes the reasons they gave for this echoed those of the first generation.

Friends happen to be Muslim, didn't select on purpose – just got on with them. Easier to have friends with similar background, similar interest and values. Talk about and do same things, satisfactory to all of us.

They also found that a common religion and ethnicity allowed them to be more open about their home life with each other.

Some topics are easier to discuss and are common to all of us, for example problems associated with parents.

Friendships of this sort were also sought because of racism. Two Punjabi students explained their isolation and despair when it came to dealing with racism, particularly racist jokes which often occurred in lectures and in everyday social interaction at university. In their isolation and to avoid arguments, they often felt they had to laugh along with such 'jokes'. They felt that such issues could have been addressed more effectively if they had had a number of fellow Asian students who could have acted as a support network.

For some, the choice of friends was a natural product of their participation in Asian culture and a conscious desire to affirm their ethnic identity. A Gujarati woman felt that if Asians were to be successful in Britain and at the same time true to themselves, they had to utilise the positive aspects of the two cultures. As a result, she had made a conscious decision to centre her life around her ethnic community, while seeking to maximise the opportunities she had in Britain, particularly in relation to education.

From the Asian side, I take my religion and culture because without it, I would have no roots and I would be lost morally ..... [and] from this country, we are taking the educational opportunities we may not have had in India.

Unlike most other second generation respondents, this woman also felt that, despite being born in Britain and going through the same education system as white people, her social interests were very different from those of her white fellow students.

When I went to college, I mixed with people from different backgrounds but still stuck together with Asian friends because I didn't get on with the English. Their interests and my interests were completely different. What they found enjoyable just didn't appeal to me, whereas what other Asians were doing appealed to me.

As an example she mentioned that her white fellow undergraduates tended to drink and smoke and, therefore, socialise in pubs, which she did not enjoy; and that she enjoyed attending 'bhangra-dos', dancing to the Punjabi rock music bands, which her white fellow students did not.

Given the foregoing, it is perhaps not surprising that most first generation respondents, although feeling it was inevitable, expressed concern at the decline of the extended family as the central focus of social activity. They appreciated that this was likely to be a continuing process as the second and third generations 'began to increasingly take on white values and live more individualistically, concentrating only on their immediate family and themselves'.

It was argued that this would have an impact on the help people gave one another, particularly when it came to helping the elderly.

In the past, people used to genuinely help each other. Today, people live far apart from one another and do not feel the obligation to lend a hand as our forefathers did in their time. I have known children to leave their elderly parents in nursing homes because they could not be looked after at home.

Some second generation respondents also acknowledged the changing nature of obligation to the extended family and one's own ethnic community.

In my grandparents' time, it was a very close-knit community and we have lost a bit of that. I think there was more a duty to help each other out. If anything like a bereavement or injury had happened in the community, my grandparents would have been at the injured family's side within the hour. It wouldn't happen nowadays, unless it was within the immediate family.

This respondent attributed the change to people being 'more selfish' and not having the sense of obligation and duty to the family that had existed in the past. She acknowledged, however, that it was also due to spatial dispersion, which made visiting each other time-consuming, and to people now tending to devote more time to their careers and education than people in the first generation had done.

Comment

Changes in family life are of course a well known feature of contemporary British society, but the evidence from our fieldwork suggests that Caribbean and Asian families may be undergoing even greater change. One reason for this is that extended family life or community-based mutual support and care structures are a more recent presence for these groups than for white British society (though see Young and Willmott, 1957).

The contrast here between the Caribbeans and the South Asians is, however, quite radical. The Caribbean respondents speak of having lost their extended family and community networks in the migratory process, whereas for the Asian migrants the extended family continues to be the central social institution. Indeed, there is independent evidence that the extended family was thoroughly involved in the South Asian migratory process through 'chain-migration', whereby earlier migrants requested or assisted the migration of others, usually kin, and arranged for their lodgings and work (Watson, 1977). There is also evidence that this process has continued in the form of 'internal migration' as Asian individuals and families move from one location in Britain to another, usually in search of work (Robinson, 1991).

Why the extended family was or is able to play such a role and survive for Asians but not for Caribbeans is too complex a question to be answered on the basis of our study, but this and later chapters suggest that Asian families made, and still make, considerable demands while giving much support to each member. It is perhaps not only that tighter structures may have greater resilience but also that they may be able to offer more advantages and needs-satisfaction and so give people more reason to support their continuation. For example, some Pakistani young women may feel that their families have more to offer them, economically and in terms of personal and social status, than they believe happens with their white British peers and their families (Shaw, 1988:163).

Nevertheless, if the comments of the first generation Asians suggest that the extended family has been integral to their way of life, the views expressed by the second generation suggest that the extended family is giving way to the immediate or nuclear family. The second generation had much less contact with the extended family which was, at least up to this stage of their lives, hardly conceived of as a support system. Much of the value, the emotional, moral and material support that the first generation placed on the extended family, the second generation placed on the immediate family, meaning parents, siblings and probably grandparents. While this means that their lives are probably more centred around the immediate family than are those of their non-Asian peers in Britain, it also means that their social life is unlikely to be centred around the extended family but based instead on relationships formed through work or educational institution.

We did not in our research explore what the immediate family might consist of. Data from the 1991 Census partly helps to fill this gap. It does not help us to plot the existence or decline of extended families and kinship reciprocity because it does not allow us to measure the relationship between different households, But by briefly examining the range of households that people live in we can give some content to what our respondents meant by immediate family. It enables us, for example, to measure the extent to which the extended family is present within a household and the extent to which the core family has shrunk. Table 1 gives the average figure for persons in a household.

In reading the census data one has to bear in mind that the South Asian population, especially the Bangladeshi, is much younger than most of the British population including the Caribbean. One implication of this is that the average Asian household is likely to be larger simply because it is more likely to have children (and Asian, especially Bangladeshi and Pakistani, fertility rates are also higher than average). Nevertheless, if we assume that in most cases household members are family members, the point is that for Asians, family means living together with more family members than it does for the rest of the population, including the Caribbeans, whose position

Table 1   Average number of persons per household by selected ethnic groups, 1991 Census

Great Britain	2.47
Black-Caribbean	2.52
Black-Other	2.51
Indian	3.80
Pakistani	4.81
Bangladeshi	5.34

Source: Census 1991 (Crown copyright)

in this respect is not different from the rest of the population. (For this and other census data presentation, besides 'black-Caribbean' we have included the category 'black-Other' for there is good reason to believe that most people within this category are of Caribbean descent, Ballard and Kalra, 1994:7.) By itself, however, average household size is a relatively crude measure of a family household. Table 2 presents the proportions in different household types.

Households with three or more adults together with one or more children under the age of 16 are for the most part households with parents, children and adult children and/or the children's grandparents. They therefore indicate the presence of extended families within households. Table 2 shows clearly that such extended family living is relatively rare in Britain, including among the Caribbean population. It is, however, found

Table 2   Household types as percentage of all households

	3+ adults & 1+ children	2 adults & 1+ children	One-parent family	Lone pensioner adult	Single non-pensioner	All other house-holds
Great Britain	5.4	19.8	4.2	15.1	11.7	43.8
Black-Caribbean	5.9	14.8	16.9	5.3	23.1	34.0
Black-Other	3.9	20.9	16.0	2.5	25.6	31.1
Indian	21.2	36.4	3.1	2.0	7.8	29.5
Pakistani	27.3	41.0	4.8	0.9	7.2	18.8
Bangladeshi	32.8	43.3	4.4	0.7	5.2	13.6

Source: Census 1991 (Crown copyright)

in large numbers among the Asians, amongst whom such households are four to six times more common tl an the average, the more so the shorter the period the Asian group has been settled in Britain.

Corresponding to this is the fact, as shown in Table 2, that relatively few Asians live alone and hardly any of them are lone pensioners, partly because pensioners form a smaller portion of the Asian population compared to the country as a whole. The predominant household with children in Britain contains two adults, except among Caribbeans, for whom it is slightly less common than the single-parent household. For Asians the two-adults-plus-children household has become the most common way of living, being more than twice as common among Asians as the national average. The fact that the most common Asian household is of a non-extended form (though of course this by itself says nothing about the inter-household character of the extended family) is an important statistical confirmation of the views expressed by our respondents. It also marks something of an irony that Asians now exhibit most clearly a form of family, 'Mum, Dad and the kids', that is or used to be regarded as quintessentially Western.

While the single-parent family is the least common way of bringing up children in the population as a whole, it has among the Caribbeans become more common than the other ways. Of equal significance is the fact that the most common form of Caribbean household is for a non-pensioner to live alone, a condition in which twice as many Caribbeans find themselves compared to the average. Taking these two forms of households together, the single parent and the lone non-elderly adult, 40 per cent of Caribbean households, as opposed to a national average of 16 per cent, comprise of an adult not living with another adult. This does not necessarily imply a state of atomism and individualism, because no data on relations of care and support between households is available from the Census (though this is a topic which is included in the Fourth National Survey of Ethnic Minorities). It is, however, a long way from the pre-migration Caribbean state of extended families and communal reciprocity, and we note that some black commentators (Dennis, 1989; Ouseley, 1993) and academic researchers (Dench, 1993) speak of 'the black family in crisis'.

Some comment is also necessary on the fact that the Census records that the proportion of Pakistani and Bangladeshi households which are one parent families is higher than the Indian and about the same rate as the national average. This runs counter to personal experience. What Table 2 really shows is the predominance of households with children amongst Pakistani and Bangladeshi households. When one-parent households are recalculated as a proportion of all households with children, the national figure is 14 per cent, while for Pakistanis and Bangladeshis it is 7 per cent and 6 per cent respectively. A suggestion also has been made to us by Roger Ballard that many of these households consist in fact of families where the father is working away from home, probably abroad, most likely in the country of origin or in the Middle East, for which the term 'one-parent family' is somewhat of a misnomer. This makes sense; the practice is not uncommon in Pakistan and Bangladesh.

Our respondents' comments show a further implication of the movement away from the extended family. This is where the extended family ceases to be the primary context for socialising and friendships because other contexts, especially work and education, become more important. A direct implication of this is the extent to which friendships are formed with people outside one's ethnic group. Thus, most of the first generation Caribbeans had non-Caribbean friends and half of that generation and two-thirds of the second generation had non-Caribbeans as close friends. On the other hand, most of the first generation Asians had friends only from within their ethno-religious community and none had non-Asian friends. While most of the second generation did have non-Asian friends, at their present stage in life, few had non-Asians as close friends. Patterns of friendship among second generation Asians, then, have undergone, and no doubt will continue to undergo, significant changes but still fall quite a long way short of the development of inter-ethnic friendships amongst the Caribbeans.

This development is mirrored in some white attitudes. There is evidence from other sources that among some white working-class groups black cultural styles are held in high prestige and friendships with young black men and women regarded as acceptable (Back, 1993) and that black-white marriage and cohabitation have become quite common (see Chapter 5). Many young white people, especially boys, admire and hero-worship successful black 'stars' in football and sport, music and entertainment (Boulton and Smith, 1992), and there is a general perception of Caribbeans as 'hard' and Asians as 'effeminate' (Cohen, 1988:83; Mac an Ghaill, 1988; Gillborn, 1991), with the result that simultaneously with the forming of black-white friendships it is possible to have a hardening of exclusion of groups like the Vietnamese (Back, 1993).

However these patterns of exclusion and affiliation may develop, they illustrate not only the changing, unpredictable nature of racism but its relevance to the formation of friendships. Several respondents, as we have shown, felt the need for close friendships with persons of their own background, or at least those who suffered a similar condition, in order to share their experience and have their support. Some respondents' remarks suggest that the subjective experience of racism, including perceived racism and anticipated racism, is closely bound up with ethnic group bonds and ethnic identity; with preference for members of one's own group and with the desire to affirm one's origins and cultural heritage. This was seen to be true not only at the micro-level of friendships but came out even more clearly on a macro-level in respect of participation in and the rationale of community organisations – organisations which owe their existence to racial and cultural exclusion but which can for some participants become the means of promoting ethnic identity. In the case of the Caribbean community networks it may well be the case that some of these are attempts to fill the place of forms of community support that were lost in the process of migration.

Ethnic identity is of course not simply a product of racism, but in the context of an environment which includes racism, ethnic identity amongst victim groups will almost inevitably be racialised, that is to say, formed and 'distorted' in response to racist categorisation, stereotypes and exclusion. Ethnicity in the form of norms and structures to do with family life has, as we have seen in this chapter, a sociological weight, a dynamic of its own, but it is a dynamic worked out in the context of other processes such as British socialisation, individualism and racism. The results of such multiple processes are not predictable and are not uniform across groups. Minority norms in connection with family and friendships shape personal and social circumstances but are also shaped by them.

3 Community Languages

Language is widely regarded as a feature of ethnicity and is indeed most often cited as the central element of peoplehood, especially in the context of European nationalisms (Smith, 1981). Minorities which have a distinct language from the rest of the population may well think of themselves differently from minorities which do not. We wanted to get some idea of the attitudes members of minority groups had to their linguistic heritage, and to what extent they saw this heritage as a feature of community identity. We asked how important it was to respondents to speak their community language, why and on which occasions; and how important it was to them that their children should speak it.

Caribbeans

Creole and Patois are commonly understood to refer to specific Caribbean languages or dialects used by people of African decent in the Caribbean and elsewhere. These languages are often misconceived by outsiders as corruptions of the English language. They are in fact descended from the languages of those who were taken from West Africa to the Caribbean in slavery, though they evolved to include vocabulary from the indigenous Caribbean peoples and European slave-masters. The African languages gradually disintegrated because of the political and structural dominance of English and European language speakers, creating a fusion of languages from which today's Creole and Patois are derived (Alleyne, 1988). While, together with the European languages, they became the common forms of language spoken by the mass of peoples in many Caribbean islands, there are wide variations, according to class and region in the languages and dialects spoken. They have a literature of their own, especially folk tales and folk poetry, in an English script. More recently, reggae and dub poetry have given the Jamaican language in particular an international exposure.

Attitudes towards the use and transmission of Creole and Patois languages among the first generation in our sample were mixed. Half of the first generation respondents felt that it was not important for them or their children to maintain an oral Creole or Patois tradition. It was felt that the use of such language was limited, as a mode of communication to other Caribbean peoples only, and would not therefore offer employment opportunities to their children living in England. These parents did not want it taught at schools alongside European languages; they saw the relevance of learning a language as mainly pragmatic, to help get an 'education' and a job.

> *It's like saying how important is it for them to speak Swahili or something like that. They are living here and now. Do they plan on going to work for an African embassy? Are they planning to go and live in Africa? How much of a benefit is it going to be for them?*

The other half of the first generation group, however, felt that it was important for their language to be transmitted to their children as part of a cultural identity.

> *Yes, they should understand, know their ancestors, where they are coming from.*

This did not mean they thought that Caribbean languages should be offered at school. Most parents felt these languages should be 'picked-up' by children at home, in an informal way. Knowledge of Creole or Patois would allow links with the Caribbean to be maintained. Children would have the ability to understand and interact more meaningfully with family, friends and others in the Caribbean. Even some of those parents who did not speak a Creole or Patois language expressed a desire for their children to be able to use such language.

First generation parents noted a decline in their own use of Patois and Creole languages. As one first generation father said:

> *I am accustomed to speaking this kind of English now. The Patois is kind of dying out in me.*

Other parents felt their children's use and comprehension was limited.

> *With my children at home, when I say it to them, they take it as funny, they laugh. Although they understand a lot of things they don't really speak it as fluent as I do, just one or two things. I try to speak it to them as much as possible.*

Both first and second generation respondents suggested that the use of Creole and Patois languages is now limited to the private arena. Such language was most often used at home with the family. Interactions with friends at social gatherings in public and in private were could be conducted with a liberal sprinkling of Creole or Patois. In general these languages would not be used at work, as respondents felt that some white employers and employees, as well as not being able to understand the conversation, would sometimes consider it unprofessional, uneducated or even rebellious. Although there were many positive attitudes towards the maintenance of such language its use was therefore limited. For the most part,it was only on visits to the Caribbean that respondents felt able to use these languages in a wider fashion. After the Fourth National Survey of Ethnic Minorities we shall have a better idea of the extent they are still in use, who uses them and with whom.

In general second generation respondents felt the importance of maintaining their oral tradition as part of a wider cultural identity. As one respondent put it: 'it is an expression of blackness'. Being able to use such languages was also considered an advantage. As well being useful for communicating with others, they would give people the ability to 'tune in' culturally within the family and other Caribbean peoples: 'It gives me a sense of identity, it gives me something I can relate to'.

A minority of second generation respondents suggested that the importance of Creole and Patois was dependent upon where a person lived and the social circles in which he or she moved. In areas where other Caribbean people were a rarity it would not be considered an essential skill. However, most second generation respondents felt that being able to communicate in this fashion was crucial. Those African-Caribbeans who were unwilling or unable to use Creole or Patois were viewed with disdain by some second generation respondents. They were somehow 'outsiders' or not in touch with 'where they are coming from'.

Many second generation respondents felt that Caribbean languages should be offered in schools alongside other majority and minority languages. These respondents felt this should be part of a wider 'cultural education' which would encompass Caribbean literature and 'Afro-centric' history. Some respondents felt cheated by their experience of education, the absence of Caribbean languages within the education system being an example of its limitations. Respondents felt that no account was taken of their desire to develop their language skills.

South Asians
The four South Asian groups each has a distinctive language:

Punjabi   -   Punjabi
Gujarati   -   Gujarati
Pakistani   -   Urdu
Bangladeshi   -   Bengali (Sylheti dialect)

Many members of these groups can understand some of the language of others. The languages share a common oral base understood in most of the Indian sub-continent and by many Asians in Britain (it is the medium which enables the Bombay film industry to reach the largest film audience in the world). But each language is at the same time separate, with a distinct script and a rich literature. The majority of Pakistanis in Pakistan, and even more so in Britain, speak Punjabi as their first or home tongue, and it is one of the principal regional languages of Pakistan. Their Punjabi is orally very similar to that of the Indian or Sikh Punjabis but while this other Punjabi is written in a script, Gurumki, derived from Sanskrit and unfamiliar to Muslims, most Pakistani Punjabis here, rather than developing a Punjabi literary language, have made Urdu, one of the national languages of Pakistan their own (the other is English).

Many older educated Bangladeshis too can understand Urdu (having been taught it prior to 1971 when Bangladesh was part of Pakistan, or prior to 1947, when Britain ruled over the whole sub-continent), but most Bangladeshis in Britain, coming as they do from the remote poor rural province of Sylhet, cannot do so, and speak Bengali in a distinctive dialect. While Sylheti has no script of its own it is sufficiently distinct from Bengali for speakers from the two languages or dialects to have difficulty understanding each other.

Languages in the sub-continent are many and varied and of different cultural and official standing. While some enjoy official national status and are taught in state schools, others have been the focus of regional or ethnic identities and some, usually following a period of political conflict, have become official languages of regional governments. Additionally, there may be other local languages, so it is the common experience for even the large number of illiterate persons to be bi- or multi-lingual. Nevertheless, there is normally one language that is the focus of ethnic pride, as are the four languages mentioned above. The four Asian groups here could, however, easily be divided into sub-groups; for example, Pakistanis come from different regions of that country and often have a distinctive language or dialect, but, in thinking of themselves as Pakistani, they are likely to give special status to Urdu.

Both the first and second generation of all the Asian groups in our sample thought the ability to speak their ethnic group language was of crucial importance in how they saw and described themselves. Three kinds of reason were given. First, it was stressed as a means of communication within the family and with other community members, especially elders. Several first generation people preferred to use their community language and had more facility in it than in English: it was an essential language for intimate communication and sense of family between parents and children, and between grandparents and grandchildren. The argument also applied to those who visited their countries of origin. As one second generation person who had been on a recent trip to India said:

> *It's hard enough to relate to people from a different country like India when you live here, it's even worse if you can't speak the language. The way you are brought up and the way they think is different but language provides that common feature which enables some sort of communication to take place.*

Secondly, the language was important as a bond of community even when each of the participants could speak and express themselves in English. Thus Gujarati first generation respondents argued that many in the community would find it insulting and offensive if other Gujaratis spoke English to them because it would be viewed as being 'snobbish' and superior, particularly if the person concerned could converse in Gujarati. Punjabi first generation respondents argued that language was important for Punjabi identity when otherwise Indians were becoming more and more alike in terms of food and dress, and religion was of declining significance for them.

Finally, some people argued that the languages in question were a key to one's cultural heritage. As one first generation woman said:

> *Our culture is enveloped around spoken Gujarati. One cannot access into our culture without being able to speak and read Gujarati.*

Another first generation respondent put the point more generally: 'If you don't know your language, you can't understand your history.' This was a view stated also by some of the second generation.

> *It is the central feature of Indianness. To be in touch with one's roots, it's vital we are able to speak the language.*

With two of these languages, a special religious significance was mentioned. The two first generation Punjabi women said that it was not only important for people to speak Punjabi but also to read it. The emergence, growth and development of the Sikh religion was closely interwoven with a form of Punjabi ethnicity or nationhood and, in addition, the Sikh religious book, the *Guru Granth Sahib,* was written in Punjabi and only those who read it could get the necessary spiritual nourishment required to live life as a Sikh in Britain.

Some Pakistanis also remarked on the religious dimension of Urdu. While Arabic is the language of the Qur'an and it is perfectly possible to be a devout Muslim without knowledge of Urdu, historically Urdu came to be the premier language of South Asian Muslims and a vehicle of Muslim rule and culture. Written in a Persian-derived script and with vocabulary from Arabic and Persian, as well as from Indian languages, Urdu has for some time been regarded by many Muslims of the sub-continent as integral to their Islamic heritage and identity. As a second generation Muslim woman said 'Urdu creates a mentality that is permeated by our religion and its values'.

Three British-born Asians thought that the desire to keep alive the Asian language and to teach it to the young should not be a high priority. These respondents felt that the ability to speak an Asian language was largely irrelevant to life in Britain. A young Punjabi pointed to the fact that the major reason why the second generation continued to speak Punjabi was to converse with elder members of their family. With the impending decline of this generation in 20 to 30 years, he said, the exercise of teaching his children Punjabi would be largely redundant because 'by that time, we'll all be probably speaking to each other in English anyway'.

Two Urdu speakers took the same view and in a group discussion argued against their peers that as a second or third language at school Urdu was of less relevance than a European language and would only encourage Pakistanis to be backward-looking rather than making the most of their present and future opportunities.

While this was a minority view, members of both generations said a gap was opening up between the aspiration to know one's ethnic language and its literature, and the implementation of these desires. For example, while a majority of the second generation said it was important to them that when they become parents their children learn to speak and write the language in question, it was evident that many second generation people could not deliver this instruction themselves. Several first generation Asians complained that there was a danger of losing these languages as the level of knowledge was not being maintained across the generations. Many second generation people admitted that they could not read or write the relevant language, and the use of the spoken language was being increasingly restricted to home and family. Sometimes the new generation of parents, already accustomed to speaking in English to their siblings and cousins, were allowing English to develop as the language of communication between themselves and their children.

The remarks of our respondents suggest that this process is most advanced amongst Gujaratis (perhaps because most Gujaratis who came from East Africa were already speakers of English and because Gujarati has no special religious significance), but has hardly begun amongst Bangladeshis (perhaps because their period of residence in Britain is the shortest) – for nearly all the second generation said they used Sylheti on a daily basis and would certainly pass on their oral tradition to their own children.

Anxiety about decline in the use of community languages has led people to engage in some counter-action. One first generation Gujarati described a policy increasingly adopted by parents.

Children speak Gujarati at least in the home as this would improve their speech and help them to communicate with our elders. They should also speak Gujarati at special functions and gatherings.

Two first generation Pakistanis had gone as far as setting up supplementary classes in Urdu to meet what they perceived as a growing need. As one of them explained:

When my children were young, there was no awareness of the importance of learning the mother tongue. That's why I set up this organisation to teach the mother tongue as a language – my children attend these schools.

Thus, while there was a general perception that there was a decline in the use of community languages and that these languages would not be essential for communication within families beyond a limited period of time, nevertheless few Asian second generation individuals were happy to see these languages disappear in Britain, even if their own facility in such a language was limited. They were moved by the arguments of community identification and cultural heritage to wish these languages to be taught to the young, where necessary through supplementary classes or through school curriculum provision. Whether this interest is enough to stem the decline is unclear but it could provide the basis for a renewal.

Comment

Some South Asian languages overlap with each other and most Asians in Britain are able to orally communicate with each other in a Urdu-Hindi *lingua franca,* though this is less true for Sylheti speakers. On the other hand these languages are quite distinct from English, unlike modern Patois or Creole, which developed out of the interaction between African and European languages, including English. The Asian first generation began with a language that was comprehensive, adequate for all contexts of community life including religion, and radically different from English, the language which had now to be acquired. The Caribbean first generation, on the other hand, were bi-lingual with English and Creole or Patois, or were monolingual English speakers. They did not regard English as a foreign language or even as their secondary language, whereas for most first generation Asians it was a foreign language and at best their secondary language.

Thus there is a sharp contrast between the two sets of first generation respondents. Several of the Caribbean first generation respondents spoke of a decline in their facility in Creole or Patois, and half of them saw no point in maintaining those languages or of teaching them to their children. The Asian first generation respondents were still active users of their own Asian language, in which most of them continued to have a greater facility than in English. Moreover, they had brought up their children to speak in the relevant community language and believed that this was an important part of their children's upbringing and cultural identity.

If the two sets of first generations present a contrast, there are convergences between the two sets of second generations. Most of the Asian second generation are bi- or multi-lingual with a greater facility in English, which may be the only language in which they can read and write; those who are monolingual will have lost the language of their parents, and others are in various stages of doing so. In this respect, being monolingual English speakers or bi-lingual with probably the greater facility in English, they resemble the Caribbean first generation. However, unlike the Caribbean first generation they are for the most part strongly committed to the view that their ancestral language is a valuable part of their cultural heritage, ought not to be lost and indeed ought to be taught in state schools.

But in this they are like the Caribbean second generation who hold virtually identical views about their linguistic heritage. Both sets of second generations clearly value language beyond its usefulness in terms of careers, 'getting on' and citizenship. They overwhelmingly see language as a part of cultural identity, self-knowledge and ethnic pride, and many of them would like their language to be taught through supplementary classes or through school curriculum provision.

A positive attitude towards maintaining a language is not always related to actual knowledge or use of language, an example being the Welsh language in Wales (Berry et al, 1987). In a study of 102 Sikh 16-20 year olds in Nottingham in the early 1980s, 79 per cent stated that they could not read and write Punjabi, and yet 72 per cent would have liked to have studied it at school and 95 per cent intended to pass it on to their children (Drury, 1992). Similarly, in a sample of 50 Asian teenagers in Birmingham, while nearly all said they preferred to speak English most of the time, 90 per cent also said they wished to learn to read and write their mother-tongue, and many were doing so, some at school (Ghuman, 1994: 51).

It is quite possible, therefore, that just at the time when these languages become of less instrumental importance, their importance as bearers of ethnic heritage may grow. Organised teaching in the community may develop and schools may find themselves under parental pressure to offer instruction in them. Hence it is just possible that some of the third or fourth generations may have a greater knowledge of the ancestral language and literature than their parents. Much depends upon how the value the respondents put on these languages is balanced against the other aspirations and pressures in their lives.

Here the contrast between the two sets of first generations may prove to be significant. For while there is no doubt of the desire amongst the Caribbean second generation for a revival of the Creole and Patois linguistic heritage, the achievement of which to some extent can be seen in some forms of reggae, hip-hop and dub poetry, the transmission of that heritage from the first to the second generation is likely to have been affected by that part of the first generation which did not think it was something worth passing on. The Asians on the other hand began with a stronger and more extensive ethno-linguistic base and with an implicit faith in its value and the need to induct their children into it, not least because it was the language they knew best and English was not spoken in the home. The Asian languages therefore probably have a stronger base today.

This is no guarantee that they may not disappear within the next couple of generations as has happened with the languages of other migrant groups to Britain in the past, such as those from central and eastern Europe, not to mention the fate of some of the indigenous Celtic languages. If, however, the second generation Asian statements about the value of their parents' language were to be acted upon, the sources of renewal are much more readily available, including community newspapers, films, songs, literature and religious discourses. For the Muslims, there is a further consideration of the extent to which they will want to continue to give precedence to ethnic community languages like Urdu or Bengali or, as some young Muslims (none in our sample) have started arguing, to demote them in favour of the universal Muslim language, Arabic, as was found among some of the sample studied by Knott and Khokher (1993).

4 Religion

In what ways does religion influence the way that members from different ethnic groups lead their lives? What do they look for from their religion and in what kind of settings do they think it makes a difference? How important is it to them that their children practice their faith or that they pass on their religious heritage to their children? These are the kinds of question we asked our respondents in order to gauge the place of religion in the various ethnic identities. Did people think of themselves as distinguished from others by religion or was it not really important to them in that kind of way? Did religion give them a personal motivation and strength that helped them to cope with the stresses and difficulties involved in their racial minority condition? Does a religion like Christianity which crosses racial boundaries have the potential to bring groups like Caribbeans and British whites together? Where religious and ethnic boundaries cross-cut each other what is the effect and which takes priority? On the other hand, where religion is part of a range of cultural attributes which marks minorities out as 'different', as with the South Asians, is religion likely to reinforce distinctive ethnic identities or confuse the issue by raising the question of belief and disbelief? In Britain in general a major decline in organised religion and religious observance has taken place in the years spanning the two generations we are studying. Has a similar decline occurred in the ethnic minority groups and if so, with what implications for community identities that have traditionally been formed on a religious basis? These are some of the larger questions that an analysis of our fieldwork can contribute to.

Caribbeans
All first generation respondents identified themselves as Christians. They were affiliated to a variety of denominations, though mainly to the 'historic' churches, including Church of England, Roman Catholic, Baptist and Methodist; only two respondents belonged to the Pentecostal Church. This more or less represents the balance between these churches in the Caribbean in the 1950s, when most of our first generation respondents migrated,

though it is now estimated that among Caribbeans in Britain only a minority now belong to the mainstream churches (Parsons, 1993: 246-7). All the members of the first generation said that religion was important in their lives and spoke of a duty to go to church.

The extent to which this duty was carried out varied. Respondents fell into two main groups. One group actively practised their faith, with weekly, twice weekly and sometimes more frequent church attendance. They were often involved in other church related activities and offices such as the choir, warden, usher, church socials and administration, maintenance and day-to-day activities connected with the running of the church. The other group went to church services on a less regular basis, ranging from once a week to once a month or less often. For them participation in occasional services was their only connection with the church. The importance of their faith often centred on the way in which it supplied them with a code of ethics. As one respondent said, it was 'being a good person, not doing the wrong things'. This morality made them reconsider thoughts and actions which they thought were 'un-Christian'.

All first generation respondents drew strength and encouragement from their faith and it was often used as a coping strategy in times of sadness and worry. One respondent spoke of getting a 'lift' from going to church which renewed her strength emotionally as well as spiritually. Even without a congregation there was a belief in the power of prayer or meditation as a way of communicating with God to overcome life's difficulties. Four respondents spoke directly of the strength they drew from prayer and meditation. Turning to God when help was needed was often the first source of support in any situation.

If I'm feeling depressed, if something happens and I'm not very pleased, rather than lashing out at somebody, I will meditate. It helps me to calm down.

This coping strategy was used in a wide range of situations. From life-threatening situations which could change lives to daily inconveniences which were frequently a source of worry and strain.

All except one of the first generation felt it was of central importance that their own children shared a Christian belief and had bought their children up to practise a Christian faith. Three women in this group spoke about religion as not just a system of beliefs but as part of a family tradition.

It's going back, my grandparents, my parents and me and them [her children] were all brought up in the Catholic way.

Christianity was essential to the smooth running and continued existence of these families. Parents made it clear that they would go to great lengths to maintain their families' religious tradition. They felt that a Christian faith would give their children a way of surviving the pressures and difficulties in life.

Just like how my Christian belief helps me. Every little thing that goes against my wishes, I don't blow up in smoke. Meditating would probably help them make the right decision.

While as parents they required regular Church attendance, readings from the Bible and striven to implant a Christian view of morals, they recognised that when the children became young adults there was little they could do.

You can introduce it to them, but it's up to them if they want to accept it, yes or no. They have their life to live.

I will have my say and try to influence them, but I have no control once they leave home or become a certain age.

All members of the second generation spoke of being brought up in the Christian religion, and required as children to attend church regularly. For some the practice of their faith developed into active participation in affiliated organisations such as the Girl's Brigade. Despite this grounding in Christianity over half of the second generation respondents, however, no longer felt that religion played an important part in their lives. This is not to say that they did not believe in the concept of God, but that they no longer participated in organised religious activities. Christianity as a way of life or a guide to behaviour was felt to bear little relation to reality. Taking part in young adult life, going to parties, experimenting with alcohol, exploring sexuality and secular entertainment were considered to be in direct conflict with the teachings of the Christian church. As one male respondent said, 'I felt that I could not live two lives'.

A minority of second generation respondents were active in their belief in Christianity. In common with the first generation, it gave them clear instructions on how to lead their lives and interact with others. These respondents considered they had a greater sense of responsibility, and it was reflected in their thought and behaviour. As one woman said, 'I know I am answerable to God whatever I do. It keeps me sane, keeps me honest'.

Those of both generations who attended church both gave and received much support and help. The church was felt to operate very much like a wide and extended family and this was felt to be the essence of Christianity.

The Church is so supportive, you don't have to go only when you are depressed or unhappy. You can go there and share good things that have happened. Christianity is warm.

47

Like her parents before her this second generation respondent was bringing up her child to be a practising Christian. This included regular attendance at Sunday School and readings of stories based on the Bible. He would be expected to attend church services as he grew older. Another mother felt that having a faith would bring her child clear advantages. It would allow him to be more in touch with his own feelings and more caring in his interactions with others.

> *It helps build self-respect and respect for other people; to know about love and not to be afraid to love; to be tolerant of other people; to live by the ten commandments, if you can.*

Like first generation, parents this mother also recognised that she had only a limited influence over the spiritual beliefs of her child and that the extent of this influence was dependent upon his age. Some time during adolescence or young adulthood her son would decide upon the importance of religion for himself: 'It will be up to him when he is older what he wants to choose'.

Unlike first generation parents, for her, whether or not her child became a Christian was not of prime importance. Believing in and practising a faith whether Christianity or Buddhism or some other faith, was however felt to be crucial.

> *It's not important which one he becomes, it is important that he does have a faith.*

Faith was seen as a necessary underpinning to purposeful and motivated behaviour, necessary for success in one's personal life and in terms of education and career. Without a faith to steer by, young people could easily be led astray by the many temptations that surround them.

South Asians

Our four South Asian groups included the three principal South Asian religions, Hinduism, Islam and Sikhism. All the Punjabis were Sikhs, all the Gujaratis were Hindus and all the Pakistanis and Bangladeshis were Muslims; the numbers in these groups were 13, 13 and 23 respectively. To attribute a religious label to them in the context of our research is to indicate no more than an affiliation by birth and upbringing, though of course this aspect of our study was to inquire into the significance of this affiliation to individuals, how it shaped their ethnic identity and to what extent were there common and different processes at work amongst these three religions. We shall, however, follow in this as in earlier chapters the generational divide because, as we show, while there are important differences between the different groups, the single biggest differentiating factor was generational or socialisation, that is to say, whether or not they had been brought up in Britain.

For the first generation the religious label was the second most often voluntarily chosen term after their national or regional origins. Nearly all of them regarded their religion as important to the way they led their lives. A Sikh man explained that Sikhism was crucial for him in laying down guidelines on how to live his life. This included observing to one's best ability the appropriate food and drink restrictions; behaving in a 'correct and moral way' in relation to women; and to putting the family above material desires. Similarly, a Hindu woman said that religion was important for her in defining the rules of how she and her family should lead their lives. This included expecting her children to remain within a close-knit family unit and not leave home until after they had got married and expecting her children to look after them in their old age.

The Muslim first generation men and women, too, placed the importance of religion on providing a moral structure to their lives. A Pakistani woman felt that Islam affected her 'whole life – particularly how the house was run'. In that phrase she was emphasising what she felt to be Islam's strong support for the institution of the family and its emphasis on modesty in living, eating and dress, and on an anti-consumerism, or control over the desire to have more and more material goods. While the attitude of Muslims had similarities with that of other first generation Asians to their religion, it was noticeable that Islam was more likely to enjoy a centrality in the lives of its followers (the two Bangladeshi women both referred to themselves as Muslims before referring to themselves as Bangladeshis), several of whom were quick to point out that Islam was more than a religion, it was a comprehensive way of life.

The importance of participation in activities directly related to their faith was also stressed by the first generation. All of the Sikhs for instance attended the *gurdwara* (temple) once or twice a month, prayed between one and three times a day and observed religious festivals and special days of ritual. The same was the case with the Hindus whose attendance at *mandir* (temple) was about twice as frequent. Most of the Muslims said that they tried to live to the standard of praying five times a day, giving alms to the poor, fasting during the daylight hours of the month of Ramadan and making at least one pilgrimage to Mecca during their life, as well as celebrating the religious festivals. It was clear that all first generation people had tried to bring up their children in their faith and expected them to follow it.

In our sample, the example of most organised instruction was amongst some of the Muslim respondents. Two of the Pakistani first generation respondents not only sent their children to religious classes but also the family would study and discuss religious topics together. One of these men detailed how his family and friends had two to three get-togethers every month in which a passage from the Qur'an was read and discussed with the children. If there were questions that the adults could not answer, they were written down and discussed with a religious official of the local mosque and answered at the next meeting of the families.

Despite their upbringing there was a noticeable difference in how the second generation, compared with the first generation, talked about the ways in which religion was important to their lives. There was also a considerable difference between our Punjabi and the other Asian second generation samples. While our samples are comparatively small (nine for each ethnic group, except Bangladeshis of whom there were six), the Punjabis were different from the others – when asked what their identity was, virtually no one spontaneously mentioned 'Sikh'. Although they acknowledged that their parents were very religious, they believed that religion was largely unimportant in the way they led their own lives. The only way it impinged on their lives was when they had to attend a religious festival or a wedding at a place of worship. When probed further, most did concede that religion would be one component when it came to teaching their children about their ancestral heritage. As one Punjabi explained:

> *I would want my children to learn about Sikhism as part of teaching them about Indian history and culture in order to give them a sense of being proud of their ancestral home.*

Only one second generation Punjabi, a woman, articulated a perspective on the importance of religion in day-to-day life akin to that expressed by most of the first generation.

> *Sikhism offers a flexible philosophy of rules and regulations which I seek to adhere to. Religion is the most important thing about myself, even more so than being Indian.*

However, this was very much a minority view among second generation Punjabis and this was further confirmed when it was found that none of the second generation, including the one member who thought religion important, attended the temple or prayed regularly.

The Hindu second generation were more likely than the Sikhs to acknowledge that religion was important in the way they led their lives. Yet it was a religion of private spirituality and a code of behaviour in terms of personal conduct. Certainly as measured by activities such as formal prayer and attendance at *mandir*, it was (at least at this stage of their lives) much weaker than with the first generations; most attended the mandir very rarely and usually only to attend a wedding. Most considered their religion to be a very personal affair and did not feel attendance at the mandir was central to their religion. As one second generation Hindu woman stated:

I don't go to the temple every week like my parents. Everyone has to find their own level of praying to achieve some sort of spiritual fulfilment.

Religion was also important in laying down a code of behaviour concerning food and drink, dress and socialising. In relation to food and drink, most second generation respondents observed the food restrictions like not eating beef, but on the whole tended not to observe the restriction on alcohol. Modesty in terms of dress was observed with second generation women saying, for example, that they would not consider wearing mini-skirts. In terms of socialising, second generation women said they would restrict their activities with friends from work and elsewhere to certain places like restaurants and the cinema and generally avoid pubs and nightclubs (an avoidance which coincides with the effect of the fear of racial harassment, see Chapter 6).

It should, however, be noted that a minority of second generation Hindu respondents, in particular men, felt that religion was not at all important to the way they led their lives, except when considering a marriage partner. Even this was important only because of the 'traditional views' of their parents and not because they believed in marrying women from the same religious group. On the other hand, even among this minority there was an expectation that if and when they had children, they would be introduced to Hinduism as part of their cultural heritage.

When asked if religion was important in their lives, nearly all the Muslim second generation replied 'important' or, as frequently, 'very important'. When asked to explain the importance, some answered very similarly to the first generation.

Islam influences how I relate to the family, ... at work. My behaviour is influenced through the sharia (Islamic law) in every situation.

Other answers suggested an awareness of Islam as an object of public debate and censure. One second generation woman noted that Islam:

provides a sense of identity. It teaches us what is right and wrong and gives us a set of beliefs. It helps one to see the world objectively and treats women better than is often portrayed.

In the group discussion, one of the most articulate participants, who was incidentally the president of the students' union at her college, forcefully argued for what she called an 'ethical' Islam. She explained that she had been taught by her father not to think of religion in terms of petty rules but as a body of ethical principles that had to be engaged with and newly interpreted in changing circumstances. She said that Islam was an ethical inspiration and source of her sense of right and wrong, of decency and civilised behaviour but she recognised that:

> *Some people would object to me saying I was a Muslim. They think a Muslim is someone who prays five times a day, has their hair tied back in plaits and wears a scarf on her head, whereas I see Islam more as a guidance on how I live my life, as opposed to a dictatorship.*

While other second generation Muslims did not make such a sharp separation between 'guidance' and 'dictatorship', nearly all said that they were not strict in the observance of the requirements of their faith. One made the point that he was 'not as strong religiously as my parents are.' When asked to explain what 'religiously strong' meant, he said 'praying five times a day, girls wearing a scarf, not going out at night and boys not meeting girls'.

Several respondents felt there was a tension between what they professed or had been taught to profess and their actual behaviour, but had no clear way of resolving it. Some felt that, having been brought up in England, they could not 'live life like that'. Others were concerned about 'not really knowing or understanding' the purpose behind the various requirements and prohibitions.

Some respondents claimed that many of their generation observed the ritual requirements of Islam simply out of family and community pressure. One woman said of herself: 'I celebrate Eid, fast and pray but it is more out of fear than faith'. In some ways the behaviour of Muslims parallelled that of their Hindu peers. For example, they were less likely than their elders to perform formal worship and prayer (*salat*) and more likely to rely upon a more personal approach (*dua*). Again, the most important everyday manifestation of their religion focused on a dietary rule (Hindus do not eat beef, Muslims do not eat pork) and on the prohibition of alcohol, though, as with the Hindus, the first rule was more strictly observed than the second. Finally, the Muslim second generation, like the Hindus and to some extent even the Sikhs, were unanimous that when they had children, they would be brought up in their community faith, though some added that they 'would not push them into it'.

The questions of what religious tradition to transmit and how to pass it to one's children raises two matters we have not yet discussed. These are the choice of marriage partner (for after all, the other parent, too, will be relevant to the child's upbringing), and the question of religious schools, a controversial topic that has in recent years become a prominent feature of public debates about racial equality and multiculturalism. We have kept these topics back, for each merits a detailed discussion of its own. We discuss respondents' views of separate religious schools in this section and discuss the relevance of religion to choice of partner in the chapter on marriage.

Religious schools

The debate surrounding separate schools cannot be divorced from the general debate on education and what parents consider most important about their children's schooling. It is within the context of these hopes and desires for their children that the views on separate religious schools ought to be seen.

Both the first and second generation respondents felt that the most important aspect of their children's schooling was that they succeed academically. If their children succeeded academically they would then be in a position to develop successful careers and take advantage of the opportunities given to them. This desire to see their children succeed was strongly influenced by their own lack of opportunities in education and their wish that their children should not have to suffer the discrimination, disadvantage and lack of job security they themselves had faced in employment in the 1960s and 1970s (Daniel 1967, Smith 1974).

> *I want my children to succeed so they can get a job which will make their life easier than ours.*

Within this context, there was no support for separate religious schools either among first or second generation Indian respondents, and some limited support from the Muslims. Most of the first generation felt that separate religious schools would not equip their children with the necessary academic skills to be able to compete on an equal basis with children from other cultures in the job market. Secondly, there was an acknowledgement that attending such schools would also be detrimental to their children's interests because they would not learn about other cultures.

> *I would rather my children attended multi-religious schools as this would introduce them to white people and their culture. We have to live in this country and to do this we must learn each other's ways and get on with each other.*

However, first generation respondents did acknowledge that this decision would mean sacrificing some of their traditional cultural values.

Our children are likely to be 'affected' by going to predominantly white schools. They would become more westernised and may forget their origins.

Yet the overwhelming majority of the first generation respondents were against sending their children to separate religious schools; they suggested that the problem could be overcome if the state schools offered their children the option of learning to read and write South Asian languages as part of the national curriculum as well as teaching them more about their culture and religion.

It was only among the Muslims that, for some, the balance of considerations was in favour of faith-based schools. All the first generation Muslims said that they recognised some value in sending their children to Muslim schools. The primary reason for wishing to do so stemmed from their desire to provide them with a stronger understanding of Islam, which would make them better Muslims and in turn better citizens of the country. Some of the first generation also mentioned that it was unjust for Muslims to be denied state support for faith-based schools, when other religions already enjoyed this right.

The population of Muslims is increasing in England. If government recognises Christian and Jewish schools, it is a necessity to fund programmes which would support the creation of Muslim schools where we would like our grandchildren to go.

Nevertheless, only two of the eight first generation Muslims said they would prefer to send their children or grandchildren to Muslim schools. The majority of first generation Muslims (who the reader ought to be reminded had been recruited through non-religious organisations) took a view similar to their Sikh and Hindu peers.

I find the whole idea of Muslim schools is wrong. Separating our children from children of other communities will mean that when the child gets to the age of 16, he or she will find it hard to mix with these children because they would know only one culture. They won't be able to communicate with anyone else.

While the same set of considerations were important to the Asian second generation as to the first, the balance was even more decisively against sending their children (or, more realistically, their children-to-be) to religious schools. While, as with the first generation, there was some recognition that such schools could play a role in the maintenance of culture, and some non-religious second generation respondents saw them as a safe environment against racial harassment, there was a strong current that such schools were positively unhelpful.

Absolutely never. I think it is pathetic to be honest – this whole talk of separate schools. If my kids are going to live in a multi-racial community, the worst thing I could possibly do is send them to separatist schools where they are going to meet people of only one type and be possibly indoctrinated or at least lose some kind of independent thought. I think it would be lethal.

It would cause more problems. I feel our generation can get on with the English and other people because we are all integrating. We try to understand them, they try to understand us. They question us over Diwali, we them over Christmas. That's how we begin the process of understanding each other and get rid of the stereotypes we have of each other.

Separate religious schools narrow the mind. They are huge ghettos. That's where racism starts –when you can only see from one side of the fence.

This hardening of attitude between the two generations was also evident in the fact that none of the 37 second generation individuals said they would choose to send their children to such schools. Two Muslims said they were attracted by the choice but, on balance, thought that multi-faith schools would be better for their children. Like the first generation, many of the second generation thought that state schools should make better provision to meet the cultural and religious needs of minorities and to include their heritage within the curriculum, though on the latter point some thought that the transmission of religions and languages was the responsibility of families and communities, and that schools should aim to maximise the skills and knowledge in students to take up career opportunities in Britain and Europe.

A final point of interest about our respondents' attitude to religion and schooling is their view on the need for single-sex schooling. In contrast to the question of religious schools, here opinion was roughly evenly divided and, while those who were opposed to single-sex schools were far less intense in their opposition, there was not an even split between the generations or within each group. The first generation were much more likely to say they would send their children, especially daughters, to single-sex schools, a position taken by nearly all the Muslim first generation. The majority of the second generation favoured co-educational schools, but some thought that there were real benefits for girls in girls-only schools.

Two benefits were cited in favour of the single-sex schools option. First, it was felt that having an all-male or all-female environment to study in would be more conducive to learning. Girls particularly, it was thought, would perform far better academically without the distraction of the opposite sex. This was confirmed by one female second generation respondent who related her experience that girls who went to a single-sex school like herself out-performed the girls she knew at co-educational schools.

Secondly, it was felt that girls at single-sex schools were not subject to unwritten restrictions on the types of subjects they wished to study, as they often were at co-educational schools. Hence, in single-sex schools they were more likely to be encouraged to study a far wider range of subjects, including subjects which would have been the sole preserve of boys in co-educational schools, such as the physical sciences and woodwork. Those who preferred their children to attend mixed-sex schools thought it better to 'expose' their sons and daughters to members of the opposite sex at an early age to ensure they could work effectively in their presence throughout their lives without undue hindrance. As one individual put it;

> *They need to get to know members of the opposite sex by talking and working with them so they will be able to survive in later life after school.*

Comment

If the Asian and Caribbean immigrants began with very different starting-points and attitudes over language, they are much more alike over religion. All the first generation respondents said they were religious believers and religion was important in their lives, and all but one had tried to bring up their children in their religious faith. They were involved in a high level of participation in religious activities and in the local organisation of their religion (and as we saw in Chapter 2 their social life and friendships were often centred around religion). If the proportion of active participants was lower among the Caribbean group, it seems to be made up by the high level of activity on the part of that half of the group who were regular church-goers. Moreover, some first generation Caribbeans no less than most Asians saw their religion not just as a set of beliefs or as a moral framework but as an important part of their cultural heritage and identity. Nevertheless, beyond this basic similarity of circumstances based on the importance of religion, a number of important differences can be discerned between the Asians and the Caribbeans, all of which have implications for the place of religion in the lives of the second generation.

First, and rather obviously, the case of the Caribbeans, all of whom in the first generation group of our respondents identified themselves as Christian, was different at the time of migration from that of Hindus, Sikhs and Muslims, for whom religion was part of their 'difference' and who had virtually no existing religious organisation and places of worship in Britain to join. From this flowed different experiences. On the one hand, the Caribbeans tried to join the existing religious institutions and had to come to terms with the fact that the Church and its congregations were of a piece with the general pattern of racism in British society. (We did not enquire into racism and the churches, but this experience is extensively documented, see Parsons, 1993: 253-4.) On the other hand, the Asians had to make a collective effort to institute and practice their faith in a radically new social setting. Our interest here is of course ethnic identity, and the point to note is that for the first generation Asians their religion was intricately connected with their status as an ethnic group or as an ethnic minority in Britain, whereas for the Caribbeans, even for those who saw their Christianity as part of their family tradition and culture, their religion was not significantly part of their sense of ethnic difference. Or more precisely, in due recognition of the distinctively Caribbean forms of Christian spirituality in both the mainstream churches and in the black-led churches which have mushroomed in the last couple of decades, while some Caribbeans may have felt culturally uncomfortable within British churches and in due course sought to establish their own churches or styles of worship, they were not marked apart on the basis of religion.

Secondly, though all the first generation respondents gave an importance to religion in their lives, there was a difference in emphasis between the Caribbeans and Asians. While both groups emphasised the importance of a moral framework and of prayer, the Caribbeans spoke mainly of the contribution of religion to coping with worries and the pressures of life, while the Asians tended to speak of control over selfish desires and of fulfilling one's responsibilities to others, especially family members. The Caribbeans did speak of a duty to attend church services, but the emphasis was largely on the therapeutic and celebratory, joyful nature of prayer, as much on its immediacy and mood-affecting quality as on its long-term contribution to the development of personality. Asians, on the other hand, spoke of prayer in terms of duty, routine and the patterning of their lives.

Thirdly, while both the first generation groups saw their religion as interwoven with family life, with nurture, trust, love, mutual responsibilities and the learning of right and wrong within the context of the family, the Caribbeans unanimously expressed an individualistic or voluntaristic view of religion. This came out most clearly in their recognition that as children became young adults the decision to practise the religion of their parents was one for them alone to make. The Asians had a more collective or conformist approach. The expectations of parents was that their children would follow in adulthood the religion they had been brought up in; not to do so was to betray one's upbringing or to let one's family down. Hence, some second generation Asians spoke of having to go to the temple for certain family or community functions; of fasting and praying out of fear of the censure that would otherwise be incurred; and of marrying within their faith communities in order to avoid conflict with their parents and families (discussed more fully in chapter 5).

Fourthly, according to their statements, the Asians' religious rules apply in a more definite way to more areas of personal and social life than do those of the Caribbeans. Many Asians but hardly any Caribbeans spontaneously mentioned alcohol, food, dress and choice of marriage partner when stating the importance of religion in their lives. It may be, however, that it is less realistic to think here in terms of a radical divide between two kinds of religion than to see the different religions as on a continuum between the poles of comprehensively rule-bound and totally liberal. Some Muslims' statements about conformity to Islamic law and Islam being a comprehensive way of life went much further than what was said by Sikhs and Hindus.

So beyond the level of sharing a belief in the importance of religion, there are some important distinctions between the first generation Asians and Caribbeans about what this importance means. It may be thought that the accounts of the second generation point to a common thread, namely an overall decline in the importance of religion in respect of each group (a phenomenon true for Britain as a whole and perhaps also for some of the countries of origin). It is true that in each ethnic group fewer second-generation than first generation respondents said that religion was of personal importance to them, and fewer said they observed the various rules and requirements, for example, the prohibition of alcohol. Most second generation respondents did not regularly attend a place of religious worship and even those who said that religion was important wished to interpret their religious traditions and scriptures flexibly.

In one sense the simple contrast between Caribbeans and Asians no longer holds for the second generation, for the two groups which had moved furthest and the least from the attitudes of the first generation, namely the Sikhs and the Muslims respectively, are both Asians, with the Caribbeans in between them. Certainly our findings in relation to the Sikhs are anomalous and should perhaps be treated with some caution. When asked how they saw themselves, virtually none of the second generation Punjabis spontaneously said 'Sikh', but in the early 1980s the Asian researcher Beatrice Drury, studying a much larger sample of 16 to 20 year old Sikh girls, found that if prompted all replied positively and half said they went to the *gurudwara* at least once a week (Drury, 1991). It would be surprising if Sikh identity had declined as dramatically as the contrast in findings suggests, especially as in the decade between Drury's fieldwork and ours there has been a secessionist Sikh movement and a military conflict in the Punjab, resulting in considerable anger against the Indian government's storming of the holiest Sikh shrine, the Golden Temple of Armritsar, and a heightened Sikh political ethnicity amongst the diaspora, including in Britain. Furthermore, commenting on his study of Asian 13 to 16 year olds in Birmingham in 1987, Ghuman wrote that 'the identity of the youngsters is tied to their religion rather than to their parents' original nationalities', and he found no difference between Sikhs and other Asians in this respect (Ghuman, 1994: 68; see also Francome, 1994:4 and Baumann, 1994).

On the specific issue of separate religious schools, it may be, however, that Hindu and Sikh opinion is closer to that of Caribbeans (though for the latter it was not a live issue) than to the Muslims. Though, of the 23 Muslims only two said they would categorically choose to send a child of theirs to a Muslim school. While we have not at present any data from a representative sample to check whether this finding may be anomalous, it should not necessarily be taken to be a surprising one. It certainly does not mean that most Muslims do not support the availability of the option of a separate Muslim school. Several respondents pointed to the injustice of the current situation in which there are state-funded religious schools for some faiths but not others. Perhaps the inference to draw is that while most Muslims, like those of other faiths, may not choose to send their children to a Muslim school, they would like the choice to be there for those who would. Moreover, the majority of Muslims, including the second generation, and in common with most Hindus and Sikhs, seem to want a greater recognition and teaching of their religion in ordinary state schools than they believe exists at the moment (Smith and Tomlinson, 1989:89).

The Fourth National Survey of Ethnic Minorities has some questions on religion and so will provide a better factual basis to explore these issues. The important point here is that in addition to the working-out of common processes that apply to the second generation across the groups, there are also differences between the groups. In connection with the specific issue of ethnic identity, the critical difference is between the Caribbeans on the one hand and Asians, including Sikhs, on the other.

In the second generation of every group studied here there is a strong sense of ethnic pride, of wanting to know about or at least to affirm one's roots in the face of a history and a contemporary society in which one's ethnicity has been suppressed or tainted with inferiority. This pride is not necessarily primarily located in a community religion, for this varies from group to group. Its significance here is that even those young Asians who do not practise their religion nevertheless recognise that religion as part of their distinctive heritage and ethnic identity and state that they wish to pass it on to their own children in at least that form (see also, Stopes-Roe and Cochrane, 1992:164). Whether, when they come to be parents, they will in fact do so or will be in a position to do so, is not material. The point is that they believe that not to teach their children the ancestral religion is to give them a reduced ethnic heritage, especially if the children should acquire an alternative religion with all the cultural connections and traditions that go with it.

For the second generation Asians, then, their parents' religion is not merely about beliefs or morality, nor even something to be negotiated for the sake of family peace or for the sake of 'appearances'; it is part of their own ethnic identity. The position of the second generation Caribbeans is quite different. While some of the first generation spoke of Christianity as an important part of their cultural heritage and identity, the second generation Caribbeans did not. Of course some of them were deeply committed Christians, but neither the minority who were nor the majority who were not made any special connection between Christianity and their ethnicity. Critically, those second generation Caribbeans who were not practising Christians did not have any non-religious positive feeling for or identification with Christianity, unlike the non-practising Sikhs, Hindus and Muslims who continued to see themselves as having a relationship, possibly an oppositional one, with the relevant religious traditions. Of course there is a sense in which non-practising Caribbeans could take the Christian background for granted and would not have had to make any special reference to it, given that it exists all around them. But this applies equally to white British non-practising Christians. That is to say that Christianity is not part of the *minority identity* of Caribbeans; it is not something that they and only they can keep alive.

The point runs deeper. We saw in the chapter on language that second generation Caribbeans are seeking to emphasise a distinctive cultural heritage, especially one which is distinctive vis-à-vis the white British. So English is taken for granted while Creole and Patois are regarded as important to a distinctive Caribbean ethnicity, something which belonged to them and for which they had to take responsibility. As with the English language, so, similarly, our second generation respondents said nothing to suggest that Christianity, including the distinctive traditions and sects of Caribbean Christianity, was a feature of Caribbean ethnicity. With Asians religion and ethnicity reinforce each other; but this does not seem to hold for most Caribbeans. They are just as likely, if not more likely, to perceive a tension between ethnic pride and Christianity. While no one in our sample expressed any interest in new sects or alternative religions, there is and has been such an interest among Caribbeans (Parsons, 1993). This has sometimes taken the form of black-led or African-linked churches. Sometimes, especially among the second generation, there are attempts to explicitly break with what is perceived as a 'white religion'. Examples are the Rastafarian movement in the 1970s (Smith, 1994), and, partly contributed by rap music like that of *Public Enemy* and Spike Lee's film, *Malcolm X,* the more recent interest among some young Caribbeans in the black nationalist style of Islam associated with Malcolm X and the Nation of Islam in the United States.

Unlike the other religions in our study, Christianity is thus not seen as contributing to an ethnic identity, except perhaps for some of those believers who seek to give their Christianity a distinctively Caribbean or black character. This of course does not mean that Christian Caribbeans necessarily see their religion in conflict with their race or ethnicity; none of our respondents suggested that. It is more likely that many Christian Caribbeans see it as ethnically neutral and that some see it as a legitimate limit upon ethnicity, and some may even consider it as providing a healthy alternative focus of identity to ethnicity, or at least to a pre-Christian ethnicity. For those Caribbeans who are Christians, their faith clearly gives them an inspiration and strength to cope, and so potentially decreases the need for other sources of self-esteem and personal dignity.

In this tension or dialectic between Christianity and Caribbean ethnicity, there is an interesting partial parallel with some second generation Asian Muslims. We have noted that in terms of the number and scope of behavioral rules our respondents' Christianity and Islam represent a polar contrast, with Christianity being the least and Islam the most demanding in terms of social rules. However, in relation to an aspect of ethnicity these two religions can sometimes be more similar to each other than either to Sikhism or Hinduism. This is in relation to being trans-ethnic or multi-ethnic.

While nearly all Sikhs are Punjabis and nearly all Hindus are Indians, Muslims stress that the brotherhood/sisterhood of Islam embraces all ethnicities equally (regardless of any ethnic hierarchies that may in fact exist at any one time or place). Sometimes this is developed into a conscious anti-ethnicity approach in which it is insisted that not only the requirements of Islam but also the 'imagined community' of Muslims (*ummah*) takes precedence over what are regarded as merely ethnic and national heritages.

No one in our sample explicitly argued this anti-ethnicism but it is certainly to be found among some of the second generation, especially among student Islamic societies, and is often argued for in the pages of the weekly newspaper, *Q-News*. A recent survey of over a thousand self-selected *Q-News* readers, 53 per cent of whom were Asian and mainly second generation, when asked to describe themselves by an ethnic identity as against Muslim, less than ten per cent chose Asian or Pakistani (*Q-News*, 8-15 April 1994). For our respondents Islam did not have this anti-ethnicism; they did not reject ethnicity but gave Islam a central place in their ethnic identity. Several people responded to the identity question by stating they were Muslims before mentioning they were Pakistanis or Bangladeshis, and nearly everybody, when asked what being Pakistani or Bangladeshi meant to them, mentioned being Muslim almost straight away.

It seems that for many of our Muslim respondents Islam is the core social identity, meaning not that it is always the most prominent aspect in all contexts but rather that all other significant identities and identity-shaping practices are not incompatible with it. This does not mean that for example all Pakistanis have to be practising Muslims, as they clearly were not in our second-generation sample. Nor were they in Steven Vertovec's sample of young Pakistanis in Keighley, who were not interested in practising Islam ('I will be a proper Muslim when I'm old' was the prevailing attitude) but were emphatically proud to be Muslims (Vertovec, 1993:30-31). For such young Pakistanis and others, Islam is at the very least a badge of (symbolic) solidarity; hence those claiming to be Pakistanis or that being Pakistani is important to them have to engage with some aspect or other of Islam, to explain how one's conduct, ethnicity and social philosophy stand in relation to it; it cannot be totally ignored by anyone claiming to have or to be re-fashioning a Pakistani identity in Britain.

Thus, if the non-ethnic dimension of Christianity works to limit or be neutral towards Caribbean ethnicity, the non-ethnic dimension of Islam is used to respond to the challenge of a Pakistani or Bangladeshi ethnicity by integrating them into a religious identity, by Muslimising the relevant ethnic identities. This can happen because Islam, unlike Christianity, not being part of the white British cultural heritage, does not threaten minority ethnic pride. By being able to draw upon a grander heritage and wider contemporary international connections than merely Pakistani or Bangladeshi ethnicity could call forth, it boosts that pride. This may be less true for Hinduism and Sikhism but certainly Islam and Muslim identity are critical resources in the development of British minority ethnic identities, though they also constrain the possible configurations that the relevant ethnic identities can take.

There are thus different ways in which ethnic identity and religion can come together or be in tension with each other. While there were substantial variations between the four religious groups, especially amongst the

British-born, religion had a particular relevance for the Asian ethnic identities, though largely as a background condition for most second generation Hindus and especially Sikhs in our fieldwork. A further relevance of religion for ethnic group maintenance amongst Asians relates to the choice of marriage partners, the subject of the next chapter.

5 Marriage Partners

Marriage is one of the principal ways in which ethnic boundaries are drawn and maintained: by a group being excluded from the pool of eligibility, or alternatively by members of a group seeking partners only from within their own group. Exclusion from the pool of eligibility, like other forms of exclusion, can be an important subjective experience in the formation of a group identity. Conversely, many minorities, including minorities such as the Jews, whose minority status has partly depended upon exclusion, have at various times, including the present, worried about too many of their members 'marrying out' and thereby threatening the continuation of the group and its traditions. Others look on 'mixed marriages' as one of the indicators of a healthy multiracial, multicultural society.

We wanted to get a sense of where the various ethnic minority groups stood on these issues, what kinds of consideration were influencing them and what they thought was the balance of advantages and disadvantages in mixed marriages.

Caribbeans

Nearly half the first generation group approved of or did not disapprove of mixed-race or mixed-ethnicity relationships. The choice of a partner was considered to be a personal, private matter between the two individuals concerned. Three first generation respondents had experience of mixed relationships, either personally or within their family. Several first generation respondents felt that relationships between different racial and ethnic groups were almost inevitable. Daily interaction in school, work and socially would make it likely that 'mixed' relationships would occur. As one first generation father put it:

> *Look at it this way, the kids are born in the country, they go to school together. It's like two people from the same background.*

Or a mother who would not be surprised if her children were to enter into mixed relationships given how much in common they have with the white British:

I think, because my children are brought up here, I don't think there is so much difference in the cultures.

This commonality with the white British was taken for granted by the second generation, who therefore emphasised context and opportunity.

Where I've been, there has been predominantly black girls there, so therefore I look at black girls. Before, when I was at school there were only white girls there, so I looked at the white girls. So I think it depends on where I am.

Above all, personal relationships were primarily conceived of in terms of being attracted to someone and the extent to which they were mutually compatible. 'If you see somebody you like, go for it, don't matter what colour, go for it.'

Over half the second generation group expressed favourable sentiments about mixed relationships. Three of these respondents had personal experience. In general, like the first generation, personal relationships were considered the sole responsibility of the two adults concerned. These relationships were based on love, mutual respect and common interests. It was the behaviour of the couple towards each other that was important.

It does not matter if you are black or white, it's about how you treat each other that counts.

It does not bother me that he is white. He is a really nice guy and he treats my sister well.

Yet amongst both generations reservations about mixed relationships were also expressed. Primarily because of a keen perception of the opposition that such relationships encounter. Other people's perceptions and attitudes (both black and white), were felt to be a major barrier.

Other people are going to try to wreck it. Anything that's different, that's not the usual norm, they hate that.

Regardless of the compatibility of the couple, others would disapprove simply on the basis that they were from different ethnic groups. Several examples of this intolerance were given:

When it's white people that find out that a white girl is going out with a black guy, it's the world's worst crime for some [white] people.

It's the stares you get when you are walking down the street. You get people looking at you.

If you are in a mixed relationship you are subjected to the general public, having abuse thrown at you.

Abuse was not exclusively from white people:

When I go to lunch with a white girl from work. A couple of black guys will say 'look at him ... coconut'.

A second generation woman raised a different kind of concern.

Black people are moving so far away from being black, mixed relationships are just adding to that process. We need black couples for our black children.

Indeed, there was one aspect of mixed marriages that aroused considerable scorn amongst the second generation. It was an aspect that did not actually come out in the discussion about mixed relationships but in another part of the interview or discussion when questions were asked about those people from their own ethnic group who are perceived as successful. Respondents felt strongly that some successful black people try to cut themselves off from other black people and feel a black partner is a handicap to them.

They don't socialise in a black environment and they tend to marry whites. They feel they won't be accepted in their circles if they marry a black person.

This was particularly resented because such individuals acted as role-models for the black community. Marriage to whites was perceived as a signal to others.

Black kids think that's the way it's meant to be [ie once you become successful you have to have a white partner].

It was not mixed marriages as such that were objected to but the connotation of superiority and disloyalty.

The term is a 'sell-out'. They forget where they are coming from.

Some first generation parents expressed reservations when their own children were involved. In general, these parents' preference would be for their children to have relationships with other black people, in particular other Caribbeans. As one father put it:

Personally, I would prefer him to be with a black girl, but he is my son and whatever he chooses, he has to make the choice and I have got to live with it.

Parents' uncertainty about mixed relationships for their own children stemmed from experiences of racism. There was anxiety that their child would in a mixed relationship not only have to face racism on the streets but within the home as well. There was a widespread feeling that, as well as from strangers, prejudice can come from within the family or a group of people previously known. Indeed, there was a recognition that prejudice could be experienced from the non-black partner. As one father put it:

When they have an argument, irrespective of whether they love each other or not, they still come out and call him a black or ... whatever, and that I can't live with.

Sometimes you will get all white people in a group and they hate black people, but you will be there and they will say 'you are all right' and it's because they know you so you are all right.

Dealing with prejudice was not the only difficulty mentioned that a couple in a mixed relationship could face. There was the fact of cultural differences and how they could make mutual understanding difficult. As one parent said:

Because of our culture we are so different from the British people. The way we were brought up, the things we believe in. Whereas I can understand someone from Jamaica and the other islands, I don't think I can completely understand the white person.

Most respondents, regardless of being in favour or not of mixed relationships, felt that the children of any such union would face particular difficulties. As one first generation parent put it:

They are mixed. They are not black and they are not white. I don't know how they would get on.

Anxieties over the identity of mixed ethnicity children was sometimes exacerbated by their non-acceptance by some Caribbeans. As one male second generation respondent said:

You might get a group of black girls who say 'you are not black, look at you, your hair is not the same as ours; you don't have the same problems'.

One of the respondents thought that mixed-ethnicity children were rather attractive, but none that mixed-race children might be favoured within the community for their lighter colour or European looks, even though this is a common perception. The concern was for possible abuse from a minority of Caribbeans as well as facing racism from some whites as a part of their daily experience. One first generation father explained:

They give these derogatory names, 'half-breed' or 'watered-down children'.

While most respondents focused on the disadvantages, two highlighted the positive aspects. They felt that mixed relationships could go some way to breaking down the barriers between groups in society. A first generation man argued that they contributed to 'harmony, bringing peoples closer together'.

This intense form of interaction would bring about increased knowledge of other peoples and their cultures. One second generation respondent suggested:

> *If there were not so many mixed relationships, then there would not be any awareness of different cultures.*

It was, therefore, hoped that mixed relationships would increase tolerance between groups and reduce individual prejudices, not least by giving non-blacks an insight into racism and discrimination.

> *For the white person marrying into the black family it makes them aware of all the problems that a black person can go through.*

South Asians

All the first generation respondents were themselves married to a member of their own religious and ethnic group, a marriage in which choice of partner had usually been made by their parents and other family elders. Where their own children were married it was within their ethnic-religious group, and where their children were not yet married it was very much their expectation that the same would happen. They justified their preference for endogamy in the following way. They doubted whether 'falling in love' was an appropriate way of identifying a compatible life-long partner and pointed to the high divorce rates outside their communities as evidence of its poor track record. Moreover, marriage was viewed as a union between two families and not just two individuals who happened to have fallen in love. Hence, one woman argued:

> *Our marriages take into consideration not only the compatibility of the boy and girl but also the families. Therefore, there would be little chance of the marriage failing.*

Several first generation respondents felt that if their children were to marry outside their community, family ties and the mutual obligations of parents and children (especially of adult children to look after their elderly parents) would be weakened. They would no longer be sharing common lives; their child, loosened from family ties, would go his or her own way. This could happen through a process of drift or the parents severing the relationship as an expression of their intense disapproval. This ambiguity is illustrated in the following remark by a first generation male:

For example, if my daughter gets married to a white man, she will never have a relationship with my wife or my other daughters. Because [she will] not be observing the same religion or culture. They are emancipated.

Another first generation male, while recognising that mixed marriages have a positive aspect of 'developing internationalism', having witnessed one at first hand, thought that this was 'at the cost of the family'.

In my own family an uncle had a mixed marriage that survived but at the expense of him having to give up his relationship with his mother, his sister, his family. That is until he died, after he died his body was shipped back to Bangladesh.

A further important concern about inter-religious marriages was that it would involve at least one partner losing or even having to suppress his or her culture and religion. As one woman argued in relation to a Gujarati marrying a white individual:

I would prefer not to see mixed-religious marriages because of the differences in our cultures. This would mean suppressing either one or both partner's cultures.

This person felt that the cultural differences, including religion, were so great and would involve one or both of the individuals having to change so much that even a marriage between a Gujarati Hindu and a Punjabi Sikh was doomed to failure. Others expressing similar concerns about the long-term strength of such marriages argued that Gujarati individuals would possibly have to change their faiths and lifestyles, which would mean that they would probably have less contact with their parents and the extended family. In effect they would have to drop out of or become marginal to their communities, and if such marriages became common this would greatly weaken the existence of a distinct community.

Then there was the question of which faith the children of such marriages would be brought up in. It was felt that the children of mixed marriages were unlikely to be brought up to practice the minority faith and would end up with no religion or the religion most in evidence at school and in the wider society. A related concern was the extent and quality of contact children of such inter-religious marriages would have with the Gujarati members of the family, in particular its older members. Particular concern was expressed that they would be brought up to speak English only, particularly if their partners were white or black and therefore communication with elder family members like grandparents would be very difficult. Consequently, it was felt that these children would know little about their Asian culture and way of life.

Finally, concern was expressed at the stigma and shame that would be brought to bear on the family by the ethnic community if one's daughter or son married a person who was not of one's religion or ethnic group. This problem was particularly acute for those people who lived in areas where large numbers of their group lived and where there was a high level of social interaction between members. As one woman argued:

> *It would be looked upon as embarrassing to the family. They would not know where to show their faces. Family and friends would refuse to communicate with them.*

Interestingly, while the first generation Muslims were if anything initially stricter about endogamy, arguing that it was a religious requirement for a Muslim to marry a Muslim, they were the only group who were open to marriage across ethnic and even religious boundaries.

First, they emphasised that, while it was not the norm and could lead to some cultural difficulties, Muslims were not obliged to marry within their ethnic group. A Bangladeshi, for example, could marry a Gujarati, a Pakistani, a Somalian, a Scot and so on as long as they were marrying a Muslim; ethnicity was not an important consideration and Islam itself provided enough cultural commonalities for individuals to be compatible and for their families to be able to relate positively to each other. Moreover, in such a marriage there would be no difficulty about bringing up the children in Islam.

Secondly, when a non-Muslim was chosen as a marriage partner, the first generation respondents thought that the marriage could still go ahead and be perfectly proper if the partner was to convert to Islam and agree to bring up their children as Muslims. One respondent restricted this option to male Muslims marrying a woman from the members of the religions close to Islam, to the 'peoples of the book', Jews and Christians. Others did not put a gender or religious group restriction upon this option. In this way, if not enthusiastic about inter-religious marriages, the first generation were willing to countenance them as long as they were seen as not so much as losing one of their own children but as expanding the Muslim community. It is estimated that there are between 10,000 and 20,000 white Muslim converts in Britain. Most of these are women, many of whom converted as part of a marriage to a Muslim (*The Times*, 9 November 1993, p.11). In the absence of a religious conversion, Pakistani and Bangladeshi first generation attitudes to mixed marriages were probably no different from that expressed by the Indians. This was evidenced by a Pakistani and a Bangladeshi second generation person, one of each of whose parents was white and who felt marginal to and marginalised from their respective Asian communities.

Before turning to the views of the second generation, it is important to note a significant development amongst Hindu and Sikh first generation respondents. Traditionally, these groups have not only married within their own religion but also within their own caste. In our sample, this attitude was strongly expressed by only one person. Most Hindus and Sikhs felt that, while their children marrying out of caste would cause them some concern, it was not an issue as long as the partner was of the same religion and there were 'similarities in lifestyles'. This development, which must reflect a coming together of castes, may be an outcome of the experience of being tiny minorities that realise they have much in common, together with the spirit of egalitarianism of British society, not to mention the desire to widen the pool of eligible partners. For one person there was a strong preference that his daughter marry a Sikh of the same caste as his family. Yet caste, and interestingly even Sikhism, was not an absolute boundary in this context. He said, for example, that because Sikhism has its origins in Hinduism, he would accept his daughter marrying a Hindu. Individuals he could not tolerate his daughter marrying included Muslims, blacks and whites.

In summing up the views of the first generation on religion and the acceptability of marriage partners, it needs to be stressed that, because none of their own children had married outside of their particular ethnic group, their views on such issues need to be treated with caution. It is not clear what actions they would take if one of their children was to undertake such a course of action. While some said they would act to prevent such a union, it is not obvious that all who said this would have done so had the situation arisen or that, having tried to prevent such a marriage, they would not have accepted it if it had after all taken place. One first generation woman probably articulated the wishes of most parents when she stated:

As long as the man looks after my daughter I will be happy and contented. Our children's happiness is the most important thing to me.

If the first generation views strongly reflected the ethos of family and religious ethnicity, the characteristic theme of the second generation views was individualism. In varying degrees most said that the choice of a marriage partner was a personal one and that the grounds of the choice were personal qualities, not group attributes.

71

It is completely up to the individuals. I am not racist and I feel compatibility ought to be the only criterion and not race or ethnic origin.

I don't go out with someone because of their colour but because of who they are personally.

Underneath such broad-brush individualism was a more complex set of attitudes, constrained by the knowledge of parental wishes and authority, by the fact of minority status and a commitment to one's religion and/or ethnic identity. Two Punjabi women and a Gujarati woman echoed the views of the first generation that they could only marry a man who was culturally compatible with their families. In the case of the Gujarati this was only a logical extension of cultural compatibility with herself:

What's important to me if I want to go out with anyone is that we get on, that we have strong common interests. I couldn't say that of a white or black person because I'm strongly Gujarati. So if I did go out with someone, it would have to be someone I could get along with and that person could only be a Gujarati.

While few of the second generation expressed such an over-riding emphasis on ethnicity, there was a wider acknowledgement that mixed religion marriages led to a dilution of the minority Asian culture. Some of the second generation felt that in a British context it would be the Asian person in a mixed relationship who would lose more, if not all, of their culture. The Asian person would certainly have to adapt his or her culture to the dominant culture. This was felt to be particularly so if the partner was a non-Asian man. The children of such relationships were unlikely to have much contact with the relevant Asian culture and community and probably only a restricted relationship with their Asian family. A few second generation persons thought these problems were not insuperable. For the chances are that the non-Asian individuals that were likely to be chosen would have expressed a willingness to learn and get involved in the relevant culture and/or religion. The Punjabis and Gujaratis seemed most open to mixed relationships and one of the former expressed his view that such relationships did not mean turning one's back on one's family and culture.

My parents would object because they feel that somehow they will not be able to communicate with my partner in Punjabi, that I will become subsumed in the English way of life and lose my Indian culture. I feel, with my views, the white people I have dated have understood this and therefore don't see a problem.

It is interesting that while some second generation Asians are developing a philosophy of mixed marriages by emphasising that the partner needs to support the ethnic identity of the Asian and the children of the relationship, some second generation Muslims, fewer of whom saw marriage with a non-Muslim as a realistic prospect, were backing down from the traditional requirement that in a mixed marriage the non-Muslim must convert to Islam. One Pakistani interviewee stressed that by requiring conversion, one unfairly 'pressed one's ideals and views on to another person'. Perhaps these two tendencies, asking one's partner to support one's own and the children's ethnic and religious identity, and not requiring conversion on the part of the spouse, are movements from different points but converging upon each other.

Only one second generation Muslim was explicitly against mixed-religious marriages, saying he 'found it strange that a Muslim could be close enough to a non-Muslim to marry them'. As with the first generation, the Hindu and Sikh second generation thought that caste was an irrelevant criterion in the choice of marriage partners, though the one individual who dissented did so in violent terms.

> *If my daughter wanted to marry someone who was not a Jat Sikh, she would be chained up. No-one has married outside the Jat Sikh caste in my family.*

The most important constraint on the choice of marriage partner for the second generation were parental wishes and parental authority. Many of those who stated an initial individualism ('it's up to the individual to decide') went on to add that they would be reluctant to embark on a process that would lead them into conflict with their parents. For one Gujarati woman, this meant that if she was attracted to a non-Gujarati man she 'would have to think about going out with him a lot more than if he was Gujarati'.

Several interviewees speculated that if they were ever faced with a head-on clash between romantic love and love for one's family, they would forsake the former. The following comments are from a Punjabi and a Gujarati woman respectively:

> *If I fell in love with an English guy, I still, no matter how much in love I was, would not go through with such a marriage if my parents disapproved.*

> *The word 'love' doesn't mean you are happy with the person. If it means losing my family, which is more important to me, then I wouldn't marry someone who was not Gujarati.*

Beyond the direct wish to avoid bringing conflict into the family, hurting their parents and being alienated from those that they loved, the second generation were also aware that a mixed marriage, especially if as a result of a loss of parental authority, would in each of the Asian communities evoke censure and a loss of honour and respect for the family of the defiant individual. This was a further important constraint upon people's choice, because it would intensify parental wrath and because most second generation respondents wished to avoid setting in motion a process that would embarrass and stigmatise their parents within the extended family and ethnic community. A Punjabi woman explained why certain relationships, including marriage to a non-Punjabi, were outside her range of choices.

> *My parents would skin me alive. They believe we should stick to our own kind. It's mainly because of the fear of what other Sikhs might say. It would entail a loss of respect within the community and the extended family.*

This caution or reluctant conformity was most in evidence with the Muslim respondents. While generally subscribing to the view that people had the right to select their own partners, for themselves they were willing to accept a marriage arranged for them by their parents (compare Shaw, 1988:212). Indeed, some had already had an arranged marriage and, of the others, while they hoped to modify the traditional set-up so that there was some space for consultation and personal choice, most expected that their marriage would be mainly determined by their parents. They thus expected it to be to someone of their own ethnic origin, quite possibly to someone directly from Bangladesh or Pakistan, and certainly to a Muslim. The only clear exceptions were the mixed-race individuals.

The second generation Punjabis' and Gujaratis' advocacy of a more liberal approach was reflected in their generally non-disapproving attitude to mixed marriages and to positive talk about 'going out with' and 'dating', and also in answer to a further question, about what the interviewees thought of someone who lived with their partner outside marriage. As might be expected, all the first ge..eration respondents disapproved of this form of relationship and so did most of the Muslim second generation. However, about half the remainder of the Asian second generation positively approved of a couple living together. Of the other half, some morally disapproved of sex outside marriage, while others thought that in the eyes of the community 'it would be worse than marriage to a non-Sikh' and therefore bring shame and a serious 'loss of face' upon their families. Those who disapproved were not necessarily willing to condemn others. One Punjabi woman whose best friend was living with a partner said:

I support her but I would not do it myself, not because it is taboo but out of personal choice. I would not sleep with someone before marriage.

Those that favoured the option of living with a partner did so for one major reason. It was felt the experience of living together would enable the couple to, in effect, undertake a trial run to find out if the partner was suitable and if they really wished to spend their life with each other. A Gujarati woman explained her view:

I think it's really important for people to cohabit before they get married because, no matter how much you think you know your partner, you can never really know them until you have lived with them.

Similarly, a male respondent felt he would not now be going through a bitter divorce had he lived with his wife before getting married. He argued that living together would have given both of them the opportunity to find out if they really wanted to marry and spend their lives together.

In the group discussion two women brought an additional twist to the community censure argument. This was the double standards that would be applied to women. They felt that if an Asian male chose to live with an Asian partner, the woman would be much more adversely judged, particularly by her own family and ethnic community. Some of the men present who advocated living with a partner were challenged by these women as to whether they would support their sisters if they chose to live with a man. Though they were given positive answers, they remained convinced that living with a partner was not a realistic option for an Asian woman who wanted to continue to be part of her community and who did not want to bring down community censure upon her family.

Comment

When the sample is considered together perhaps the single biggest division is between the first generation Asians and the rest, with the second generation Muslims straddling the space in-between. For the first generation Asians the choice of marriage partner is probably the most important decision defining and maintaining ethnic and religious boundaries – distinguishing the 'insiders' from the 'outsiders'. Among them there was very limited acceptance of the idea that their children might marry outside their own community (see also, Stopes-Roe and Cochrane, 1990:158).

For them such a prospect raised difficulties and problems with hardly any countervailing advantages. It meant the weakening of the family as an elders-led, closely-knit, mutual self-help unit upon which they would be particularly dependent in their old age. One could say, that having materially and emotionally invested in their children, they would be seeing that 'investment' put at risk. They saw mixed marriages as meaning cultural dilution for their children and ultimately the abandonment of their heritage. They expected a loss of face in their community circle as a result of community disapproval which they did not criticise but took for granted: the community would only be applying a norm to which they themselves subscribed. For all these reasons, and in the light of remarks made by some of the second generation Asians, it seems clear that parents continue to exercise considerable control over their children's choice of marriage partner, though there is also evidence of a willingness to compromise and adapt.

The first generation Caribbeans were much more mixed in their views on the topic, with nearly half approving or not disapproving of mixed marriages, regarding them as an inevitable outcome of a common social and cultural life in which the second generation of all groups participated. Some respondents were positively in favour of them. The majority of the first generation were less sanguine, feeling that cultural differences and especially the racism and prejudice that a mixed-marriage couple and their children would face from white and black people meant that mixed-marriages were best avoided. But they did think that the choice of a marriage partner was up to the individual.

This was a proposition that few second generation Pakistanis and Bangladeshis wanted explicitly to argue with and some wished to affirm. However, except for those who were of mixed-ethnicity and therefore whose parents had had a mixed-ethnicity marriage, the expectation of nearly all the Muslims was of a marriage to a Muslim, probably of the same ethnic group and within a parentally-approved framework. In some of their stated views they were similar to the first generation Caribbeans but in their acceptance that their actual choices would be circumscribed by parental expectations they were actually closer to the first generation Asians than were the first generation Caribbeans.

The second generation Caribbeans and Indians were more positive about mixed marriages, the majority not seeing such marriages as the problem but rather other people's attitudes as creating an environment of intolerance towards the couple and their offspring. For these groups the important facts were individual freedom, personal compatibility and the quality of personal relationship as judged by the people concerned, rather than any crude assumptions of ethnic matching. The Caribbean respondents, however, seemed to see racism from whites as the biggest problem, while the Indians gave priority to justifying mixed marriages against the criticism that they led to a detachment from family and community, to cultural drift and assimilation. There was, however, one context in which ethnic solidarity was strongly mentioned by the Caribbeans: their concern that successful, high-profile Caribbeans in taking on white partners were projecting a poor community image and were acting as negative role-models to the point of racial betrayal. Yet the Indians felt the need to argue that mixed marriages were compatible with ethnic identity in the way that few Caribbeans did. Not surprisingly, therefore, the second generation Indians who dissented from the majority of their peers and argued that mixed marriages were not an option for them appealed to the importance of cultural compatibility and the desire to place their happiness within the happiness of their family rather than above it.

Taking all the second generation Asians together, one could summarise that the most important perceived constraints on the choice of marriage partner are parental wishes and parental authority, the latter not being without its negative or fearful side. This comes out when we consider not just stated views but also actions. For though more than half of second generation Caribbeans and Indians expressed no objection against mixed marriages, when we look at the statistics on mixed race marriages, one of the few topics discussed in this book on which quantitative data is available, the picture for these two groups is quite different. In fact the position of Indians is not remarkably different from that of other Asians.

Table 1 **Percentage of married or co-habiting men whose partner was a white woman, by ethnic group and age**

Age of man	Caribbean	African-Asian	Indian	Pakistani	Bangla-deshi
16-24	52*	0*	8*	9*	18*
25-44	36	4	10	7	11
45-69	20	3	8	5	1

Source: Labour Force Survey, 1988-1990

* Asterisk denotes a relatively small cell size and therefore the need to treat those figures with caution.

Table 1 presents by ethnic group and age the percentage of married or cohabiting men whose partner was a white woman in the years 1988-1990. Table 2 presents the data in the respect of ethnic minority women married or cohabiting with a white man. They contain, incidentally, sets of figures for African Asians, a group which in our study is included among the

Table 2   **Percentage of married or co-habiting women whose partner was a white man, by ethnic group and age**

Age of woman	Caribbean	African-Asian	Indian	Pakistani	Bangla-deshi
16-24	36*	0	9	2	2*
25-44	29	6	6	1	1
45-69	9	1	2	0	0*

Source: Labour Force Survey, 1988-1990

*   Asterisk denotes a relatively small cell size and therefore the need to treat those figures with caution.

Indians. The figures for the youngest age group (ages 16 to 24) are based on small cell sizes and so should be interpreted cautiously. Even so, it is clear that, while significant proportions of Caribbean men and women are increasingly in mixed relationships, and the analysis of these relationships by age suggests that the proportions are increasing, the number for each of the South Asian groups is small. In so far as there are exceptions to a standard Asian pattern, it is that there may be a more significant growth in the number of Bangladeshi men in relationships with white women (though this figure, based on a small cell size, has to be treated with caution), and that more Indian (but not necessarily African-Asian) women are having mixed ethnicity relationships than other Asians. Moreover, analysis of the 1991 Census data on cohabitation shows the figure for South Asian women to be uniformly small and as yet shows no generational difference (Heath and Dale, 1994:11; for confirmation of male double standards, see Francome, 1994:13-14).

In contrast, Table 1 suggests that choice of a marriage partner is declining as an ethnic boundary marker for Caribbeans and that, whatever racism mixed Caribbean-white couples are experiencing, it is not slowing down the growth of mixed relationships. A result of these relationships may be that some Caribbeans are increasingly coming to see themselves as part of white society on a personal level, while some white people may feel themselves in a sense part of the Caribbean community. If this does not directly happen through a mixed relationship it could happen through parenting the off-spring of such relationships. At the very least, unless present trends are thrown into reverse, the number of mixed ethnicity children will grow and they will form a significant proportion of the relevant age cohort of Caribbeans.

In terms of the topic under study, these developments suggest that Caribbean identity will become even more complexly characterised and that mixed ethnic identities will become a more prominent feature of minority identities, with perhaps mixed ethnicity people seeking to emphasise their distinctive group experience rather than be seen as marginal members of other, larger groups (Tizard and Phoenix, 1993). This is perhaps being anticipated by social theorists who characterise minority identities as hybrids, as 'new ethnicities', harbingers of a new progressive multiculturalism to which old racial divisions are giving way (Hall, 1992).

The quantitative data in respect of South Asians and mixed marriages suggests that current practice may be lagging behind attitudinal changes and may even represent 'a lull before the storm' as attitudes formed in the context of modern youth culture meet head on pre-modern forms of family life, for there is a marked difference between parental expectations and second generation aspirations. Stopes-Roe and Cochrane too, in their comparisons of parental and children's attitudes to who should choose the marriage partner and who should be consulted, found that the attitudes of the two generations were out of harmony, especially amongst the Hindus and Sikhs (see also Francome, 1994, though his sample is disproportionately middle class). They found that a quarter of the young Muslims, a third of the young Sikhs and nearly half the young Hindus expected a less traditional arrangement than their parents expected to allow them (Stopes-Roe and Cochrane, 1991:36).

While this may initially suggest that Asian families are experiencing or are about to experience serious internal conflict over marriage and related matters, evidence from the same survey suggests otherwise. When it comes to the crunch, conflict is avoided by the children accepting their parents' authority and, to a lesser but perhaps growing extent, by parents modifying traditional arrangements by incorporating some element of consultation and compromise with the children. Stopes-Roe and Cochrane report that, despite the less traditional views of the unmarried, of whom only 11 per cent expected their marital arrangements to be traditional (ie with the parents choosing a suitable partner), among their recently married peers two-thirds had marital arrangements classified as 'traditional' and the arrangements of all but 4 per cent of the remainder were 'modified traditional'. This suggests that young people's views about how their marriage partner should be chosen usually give way to their parents' views, who in a majority of cases select the partner. In our fieldwork too there was more evidence for family loyalty and reluctant obedience, especially amongst the young Muslims, than of conflict.

There have been predictions of an impending generational conflict over sex and marriage among Asians since studies in the 1970s first showed a gap between young Asians' professed views about romance and their non-romantic behaviour (Hutnik, 1991:121-122). Hutnik has argued that some of the indications of this conflict should be psychological problems among the young and a sense of alienation from their parents and their culture. Yet there is no evidence for these developments; indeed various studies show that 'youth rebellions' among young Asians are short-lived and that they do not suffer from 'culture clash', identity-confusion or low self-esteem (Hutnik, 1991:122-123; see also Stopes-Roe and Cochrane, 1990:194-204).

Certainly, the findings of this chapter reinforce the findings of earlier chapters that parental authority and family cohesion have not yet been displaced from the centre of Asian cultural life. If anything, perhaps too great a burden is being placed upon parental authority, as teenagers and young adults cannot bring themselves to agree with the content of their parents' views but want if possible to go along with their parents' wishes. In any case the point at which negotiated change is taking place is in the distribution of influence and power in arranged marriages as a decision-making process, rather than in relation to mixed marriages. Most second generation Asians were cautious about engaging in relationships that would take them and their children away from their cultural roots. Endogamy therefore continues to be prevalent and while in some instances, mainly to do with caste, the group boundaries are shifting, nevertheless marriage continues to be a principal means of affirming and maintaining an ethnic identity amongst the South Asian groups.

Stopes-Roe and Cochrane concluded their discussion of choice of marriage partner by saying of their young Asian sample:

> *They valued their kin and culture more than the freedoms which are supposed to be so desirable (Stopes-Roe and Cochrane 1991:52).*

As we have seen with our sample these freedoms are becoming desirable for some Asian young people and, if all who are attracted to them in some degree or other do not take them up, this is because parental authority and the desire to avoid conflict within the family and disgrace within the community are still powerful forces in maintaining cultural practices and ethnic boundaries. Yet within these limits the young people are seeking modifications which allows them some, and possibly the major, role in the process of selecting a partner.

6 Difference, Commonality and Exclusion

There has been much debate about how various groups of non-white British people conceive of themselves, about how they should conceive of themselves and about what language should be used when talking about them. Labelling oneself and others, and contesting labels, are at the heart of group identities, of emphasising distinctiveness and connections with other people. Debates about group labels are also relevant to how groups evoke the symbolic power of a discourse, engage in innovation and create the possibility of new social movements.

Having looked at a number of dimensions of ethnic identity through people's attitudes to different aspects of cultural heritage and through their behaviour, we consider in this chapter the issue of identity directly and in its most symbolically potent form. Respondents were asked what they saw themselves as, what group labels they used to describe themselves, and how they thought others described them. We further asked respondents how they thought their ethnic group was different from and similar to other ethnic minority groups. Finally, we sought some rough measure of our respondents' sense of identification with the white majority, their sense of similarities to and differences from this majority, and an idea of their concept of 'Britishness'. The questions posed were: What does being British mean to you? Who is British? Are there barriers to being/feeling British and, if so, what are they? Are your children more British than you?

Caribbeans: identifying one's own and other ethnic minority groups

Both first and second generation Caribbean respondents used the term black as an identifying label. Of the eight first generation respondents interviewed individually, seven used the term West Indian and six the term black in describing themselves. Most of these respondents indicated that terms such as West Indian, black, black West Indian are used interchangeably, depending upon who they are talking to and on the context. The second generation group used a wider number of terms in describing themselves. West-Indian, black, black-British, English-Caribbean, Afro-Caribbean, Caribbean, African-Caribbean and African were all mentioned. Black, however, was the predominant term used by second generation respondents. Although respondents recognised it was often used in a restrictive and negative fashion within the wider society, they saw black as a positive identity. Some respondents felt there was little point in adding any more information over and above black when defining oneself. As one respondent said: 'in the eyes of white people it does not matter where you are from, you are black'.

Black-British and English-Caribbean were less popular, with less than half of second generation respondents using either hyphenated term.

Two respondents, one first and one second generation, resisted the 'racial' labelling process altogether. One felt it to be a dehumanising mechanism. It was a process which detracted from her many experiences and varied history.

You get used to calling yourself black and not a person. They call you a colour first and then a person.

This experience was considered the product not only of being an ethnic minority but a minority continually distinguished on the basis of colour.

Having to always go out into the street and at some point you are reminded that you are a black person. Your are different until you come back in your house and you are normal again.

A second generation respondent spoke of 'being robbed' of the positive experience of being a part of the majority, being able to blend in, being just like everybody else.

In Antigua you are just another person, not a colour, not a race, just a person because you are a majority.

The Caribbean was mentioned by a number of second generation respondents in this context. For many, visits to the Caribbean had been their only experience of not being singled out on the basis of colour. Although it was recognised they were often differentiated on the basis of their accents or the clothes they wore, nevertheless not being perceived as 'different' by the majority, and feeling a part of the larger, wider group tended to happen only in the Caribbean. It was only in the Caribbean that 'black' was recognised as embracing a natural diversity, as an unremarkable feature.

If you were in Barbados they would just see you as a person because it is predominantly black, whereas here it's not.

In Britain, they are reminded in their daily lives they are black, different, 'other', and this has come to affect deeply the ways in which they define themselves. For this group, regardless of which island they were born in, where they spent their formative years or where their culture and ancestry stemmed from they tend now to define themselves as West Indian. Island identities tend not to be their first term of reference when conversing with non-West Indians.

Our culture is from the West Indies. I was born in the West Indies. I am still a West Indian.

It was most commonly in the company of other West Indians that subjects identified themselves with the use of island labels. It is often only other West Indians who are considered able to appreciate and acknowledge the cultural and historical differences between the Caribbean islands and their peoples. There was a general feeling that some sections of the white, British majority considered that all black people in Britain had migrated from the same country. As one respondent put it:

If they know somebody from Montserrat, then every black person is a Montserratian. If they know somebody from Jamaica, then every black person is from Jamaica.

National identity tended to be used when a person's island nationality was directly probed or when others were mistaken about where they came from.

Somebody looks on you and thinks you are African or .... I will say I am a Jamaican because I don't want you to think I am from another island. So I do define myself as a Jamaican, but only when people confuse me with other ethnic minorities.

Only one first generation respondent automatically used the term 'British subject' in describing himself. Another used the term 'Afro-Saxon' as a way of summing up the totality of her history and experiences which make up her identity: 'of Afro-Caribbean and English descent'. This was not a person of 'mixed parentage' but a person of 'mixed heritage'. For this respondent ethnic and 'racial' amalgamation within the family had occurred on a number of occasions. The earliest examples were through the process of subjugation and slavery. It was this mixed description that summed up the uniqueness of her historical identity. Africa as a place of descent in the historical past was mentioned by three respondents, one of whom was first generation. Only one of the second generation respondents identified herself as an African, and then with some qualification.

I do see myself as a black West Indian first of all and then secondly an African.

Self-categorisation for second generation respondents was rarely related to where they were born or where they grew up. They defined themselves within a Caribbean heritage from their parents. On the whole they did not refer to themselves as British or English when conversing with British or English people. Caribbean or Afro-Caribbean were popular choices among the 13 members of the second generation group. Ironically, the exception to this was on visits to the Caribbean. In these countries second generation respondents were more likely to refer to themselves as British. One respondent spoke of using an island identity until experiencing that she was perceived as 'other' by nationals living in the island in question.

I used to [call myself Antiguan] until I went out to Antigua. When I went out there they used to call me 'English girl'. Then I had to step back and say, who am I really?

A similar sentiment was expressed by a first generation respondent who spoke of 'not fitting in' and being called 'Englishman' by friends and family in the West Indies. A number of second generation respondents who did not use an island label recounted similar experiences. It was perceived as ironic that their 'Britishness' was recognised in the eyes of Caribbean nationals, whereas these very same features of Britishness were consistently denied by the white majority in Britain.

Respondents often felt that success for some people had become linked with a loss of some or all of their ethnic identity. Some felt that successful black personalities had disassociated themselves from their 'blackness'. They were unhappy with the idea that the only way to be successful was to 'blend in', which often meant being as similar as possible in behaviour, language, dress and aspirations to a section of white middle-class British society.

The only way to get on is to blend in with white people. You cannot be yourself because white people are frightened of black people doing that. They see it as a threat.

Interacting in white groups was interpreted by some respondents as proof of a lack of 'blackness'.

Some get educated and integrated totally in white society, forget their blackness, they become a coconut.

There was much discussion around 'letting the side down' and 'uncle Tom', and the suggestion that successful black people tended to marry whites (see Chapter 5). Many felt this loss of an identity was a high price to pay for success and would not always guarantee acceptance in the white community, hence both groups were losers.

White people will never get to know what black people are like. Black people will always be scared to show a side of themselves in case something happens. No matter how much a black person disassociated himself from his blackness, white people will never accept him, because first and foremost he is black.

The experience of being migrants was highlighted as a major commonality between South Asians and Caribbeans. However, for one first generation respondent this was the only similarity: 'The only thing we have in common is that we are all foreigners.'

Caribbeans and South Asians alike had travelled from parts of the old British empire to the 'mother country'. Both had experienced discrimination and were perceived as 'Other' by some sections of the white, British community. Whatever the other differences between these groups may be, it was argued, at least one issue, racism, brought them together.

Whenever there is a racial issue that comes up, Asian people will say we are black together, more often than not it is divided ... like African or West Indian, you are black, but the Asian, I don't know where they class themselves, but if there are any big racial issues they will come together.

Five first generation respondents felt some commonality between themselves and South Asians. Some of these expressed a notion of a shared black community.

We unite together as people. We use their shops, we support them in whatever they do in the community.

Second generation respondents were more likely to feel that minority ethnic communities were united through the experience of discrimination and exclusion from some sections of the white, British community. For them the notion of a shared 'black' identity was based on a shared experience of racism.

We are all 'of colour'. An Asian person may be accepted as a black person in certain situations; they will never be accepted as a white person.

Some second generation respondents saw the experience in Britain as a continuation of a relationship in the Caribbean. They spoke of the arrival of Indian indentured labour in the West Indies as the start of a long history of cultural mixing and in some cases common ancestry. One respondent spoke of the rich and varied heritage of many descendants from the Caribbean.

In one family it is not uncommon to have one part which is Indian-looking and another part which is African-looking. There are a lot of mixed Indian/African-Caribbean families. We are all brothers and sisters.

While cultural dissimilarities between South Asians and African-Caribbeans were referred to by most respondents, cultural similarities were also mentioned, for example, in connection with food and the family. They were perceived as groups which had similar cuisines, enjoyed food and took care in cooking. The importance of the family as a social structure which bound groups of people together out of obligation and reciprocity was another parallel drawn between the two minority ethnic groups.

Four first generation respondents felt that there were no commonalities between Caribbeans and South Asians living in Britain. Ways of life among the two groups were perceived as very different. Contrasts tended to focus on language, food, religion and dress; differences in levels of ownership of small businesses was also noted. A minority of respondents suggested that some Asians had 'held on to', and were still extremely involved in, cultural activities as part of their daily life, whereas Caribbeans had adapted and developed their cultural habits to 'fit in' with British society. One first generation respondent felt that some South Asians had more in common as a group with black Africans as both groups outwardly displayed and adhered to cultures which were very different from the British one.

Their language and dress is still kept, they are more like Africans who have kept their culture. People from the Caribbean never had that, they had to adapt.

Only one second generation respondent echoed a similar sentiment, feeling that Caribbean culture had adapted and evolved in Britain.

Their language and culture is still kept. People from the Caribbean never had that. They came here and are just a different colour, but culturally they are the same as white people.

Culture, ways of life and behavioral codes were felt to be the main features of difference between the South Asian and Caribbean communities. Most of the second generation respondents felt that religious beliefs held by Asians were a central feature of this perceived difference. Asian cultural life was considered to be centred upon religious beliefs, with religion providing a basis of social support and social cohesiveness for some Asian communities.

Places of religious worship are places they [Asians] can gather and keep community going.

Two second generation Caribbean respondents felt that many of the cultural habits were a generational product. They felt that many cultural beliefs were changing in the second and subsequent generations, with these later generations less likely to hold on to distinctive practices, cultures and religions. One respondent felt that the young had more in common than their respective parents. The experience of growing up and being educated in Britain led to commonalities in social activities and aspirations.

Most first generation Caribbean respondents, then, felt they had little in common with Asians in Britain, with the exception of the common experiences of migration and racism. Living in the same areas and working together were also mentioned. Second generation respondents were less likely to mention Asian insularity as a key difference between the groups and were more likely to recognise the basis for solidarity with South Asians out of a common colonial history, the experience of racism and youth culture.

Caribbean perceptions of Britishness

The majority of both first and second generation respondents felt they had much in common with white British people. Similarities were not simply in terms of living in the same society. Common ground was perceived to encompass many cultural habits. Caribbeans felt that they shared common attitudes, aspirations and behaviour with much of the white British majority. As one first generation respondent said:

We grew up as a Jamaican but as a British subject. We were British through and through, everything was British.

Another first generation person, describing the situation today said:

We abide by the same laws, eat the same food, work together. We are a part of them.

Most respondents of both generations, when asked who was British, said they were British. In doing so some referred to the possession of a passport, others to the place of birth, as did this second generation man:

Who is British? I am. Anyone who is born here. British is not a colour. There is no singular British identity. It's simply a birth place. My parents were born in Montserrat and so they call themselves Montserratian. Their own parents may have been born in Africa, but my parents do not call themselves African.

Others emphasised how they lived or had been formed, including this British-born man:

Those who have lived here for a certain amount of time, from the ages of ten to 20, because that is the main socialisation or social development period, which sets personality for life, you create an identity within those years. You become British if you are here then. If you grow up in another country you have a stronger identity born out of the culture of that country.

Most respondents said they felt British, and the British-born in particular felt that their way of life was of a piece with the rest of British society: 'for the second generation the only difference is the colour of our skin'.

The significance of this difference lay in the fact of non-acceptance and exclusion. As one respondent explained:

We try to live British, but we are not accepted as British.

Regardless of her efforts to fit in, this respondent felt she was still not considered British by most white people. For her, the effort of assimilation had led to frustration.

Being black and British was felt by some respondents to be a contradiction. Notions of nationality based on legal definitions were felt to be meaningless if they were not widely recognised by other members of the white community. Being born in Britain and possession of a British passport was not enough to be accepted as British.

On paper if you are born here you are English, but we 'know' that an Englishman cannot be black.

The following remark made by a respondent born and raised in England exemplifies many of the sentiments expressed on the meaning of being British, that for some white people, being white is somehow inherent to being British.

White English people cannot accept the notion of a black Englishman or woman. If you are black they do not accept you as British, even if we are here for another 100 years. White people don't see me as being British, I am always made conscious of that.

This non-acceptance did not just occur amongst strangers. Friends and partners had been known to display similar feelings. One second generation respondent went on to give a personal example of a couple in which the white British female refers to her black partner as Bajan. While it was recognised that this ascription of Barbadian origins was not meant to be pejorative, it was nevertheless felt to be incongruous as her partner was born and had always lived in Britain and culturally had more in common with her than people in Barbados.

Both first and second generation respondents talked about the non-acceptance as British on every level: from employment to personal relationships, from racial harassment and racial attacks. Two respondents gave personal examples of racial harassment or attacks that had occurred in the previous 12 months. One of these was a case of verbal racial abuse; in the other a Caribbean woman had a brick thrown at her, breaking her car window, whilst also being racially abused by a white man. A police officer was called but refused to take any action, suggesting that she contact the perpetrator herself, and the incident escalated after she called her brother to help, leading her brother to be threatened by a knife by the perpetrator and temporarily arrested by the police (for a full discussion, see Virdee, 1994). Incidents like these were behind the view of some respondents that the police and other organs of the state reinforced rather than combatted racism.

For those who had not been subjected to racial attack or harassment in the previous year the knowledge that others were caused much anger and distress. As one person put it:

When you hear of racial incidents you think, is this what they call British? I don't want to be associated with it. But then I think, this is my country, this is where I belong and I have every right to be here.

Mixed feelings of this kind were shared by many of the second generation. They are British because this is where they were born, but they feel they were not accepted as British or given the same rights and opportunities as white British people. There is therefore a persistent dilemma of whether to respond to the exclusion by insisting on one's Britishness or to write off such a concept and focus on an alternative identity.

The invisibility and 'exoticisation' of Caribbeans in the mainstream press, television and radio was also mentioned. Respondents drew attention to the notion that Caribbeans will be typically found in adverts for 'tropical' drinks or types of alcoholic beverage that advertisers want to associate with the notion of a tropical paradise. When it came to products used in everyday life, however, the same actors and actresses were rarely used. These stereotypical roles in advertisements reinforce feelings of exclusion.

Everything is geared towards white people, the TV, the newspapers, you don't see black people. If you saw them more in the media you might think yes, I am British and I do belong in this country.

Not being seen or taken seriously in the media was one type of non-acceptance; a lack of black British role-models outside of sports and entertainment was another. For one respondent being British was not possible without a re-evaluation of the past. The celebration of Britain's colonial and imperialist past was distasteful without the recognition of its effects on the Caribbean and on its African peoples. It was, therefore, impossible for her to be British if she could not identify with the signs and symbols of what, for her, it is to be British.

> *Rule Britannia, Britannia rules the waves. Britons never, never, never will be slaves. Bull-shit, we were the slaves!*

She could not 'belong' until the white majority openly recognised its racist past and the effects this had on both its white and black citizens.

There was, then, difficulty in feeling British, being British and using British as an identifying term. The feeling of 'belonging' was essential; yet how could you belong if you were not accepted and were continually excluded.

> *I have never considered myself as British. Although I have lived in Britain all this time, I still don't feel as if I belong.*

Many of these migrants from the Caribbean and their children, most of whom were born here, felt they had been consistently denied a sense of belonging in Britain.

> *It's a feeling, you should feel comfortable. It's like if I go home, my house now [in London], this is my home now and I feel belonging within my walls. I should feel that on the street. I don't feel that belonging within this country.*

> *If there is an old white lady I will say to her would you like me to help you across the road. I won't just grab their hand because they might jump and think that I am going to mug them. If it's a black lady I will just take her by the arm, because I know she won't be afraid of me.*

It was not only strangers but also friends and neighbours who were sometimes overly cautious in their interactions with Caribbeans. Some respondents felt that it was only on the superficial level that some sections of the white majority interacted with them. At least one respondent felt that on deeper and more personal levels barriers were put up. One first generation mother felt that acquaintance was permissible but 'serious' long term relationships were out of bounds. Acceptance went as far as the front parlour.

> *They come in for a cup of tea, but that's as far as it goes. The day your son wants to marry their daughter its a different story.*

Some respondents suggested they felt British only when visiting other countries because of their ownership of a British passport. Visits to the

United States and the Caribbean were mentioned by a number of respondents in this connection. However, it was not just the passport but also the type of language thus used and their British accent that identified them as British or English to residents of countries outside Britain. This often came as a surprise, especially for second generation respondents. They were assumed to be and were labelled as – 'British' or 'English' in a way they feel they almost never are in Britain.

South Asians: identifying one's own and other ethnic minority groups

As with the Caribbeans, each of the South Asian group offered a variety of terms in answer to the question of how they would describe themselves. All four of the first generation Punjabi Sikhs described themselves as Indian, as did several of the second generation, though some said Asian, others British Asian or British Indian. Of all the Punjabi Sikh sample only one referred to himself as a Sikh. This is surprising given the recent period of political alienation of Sikhs from the Republic of India but in line with our discussion of the Sikhs' comments on religion (Chapter 4). Only one first generation Gujarati referred to himself as Indian; the others described themselves as Hindu Gujarati, as did several of the second generation, the others variously describing themselves as Asian, British Asian, British Indian or just Gujarati. Perhaps because of their East African origins (most of the East Africans are Gujaratis) or because of a stronger Gujarati or Hindu identity, Indian was less of a primary identity amongst the Gujarati than the Punjabi sample. It is worth noting, however, that nearly all of those with East African origins chose 'Indian' in filling the 1991 Census form rather than opting for 'Any Other Ethnic Group, please describe' (Ballard and Kalra, 1994:5). Two first generation Pakistanis described themselves as Pakistani Muslim; the same categories were used, roughly in equal proportions by the second generation. The only Pakistani to identify himself as Asian was a person of mixed ethnicity. The first generation Bangladeshis were evenly split between the terms Bangladeshi and Muslim, which were also used by the second generation, though British-Bengali was equally in use. None of the Bangladeshis described themselves as Asian in the context of first descriptions, though several identified with it later in the interview or group discussion.

Most South Asians, then, identified more with an ethnic or religious identity than with being 'Asians'. A pan-Asian identity was present but it was far less secure and taken for granted than the pan-Caribbean identity was among the Caribbeans. They were just as conscious of differences between Asian groups as they were of similarities, which many, especially

91

among the first generation, thought relatively superficial. Sikhs and Hindus were more likely to say that they had similarities with each other than with the other Asians; and, similarly, Pakistanis and Bangladeshis were more likely to point to their sharing the same religion as a fact of inter-group similarity. As well as religion, language was listed as a basis of difference, as were dress and cuisine. Those who thought there were similarities between Asians emphasised the fact of religion-centred cultures based on similar family structures and moral codes. All were conscious that the similar physical appearance of Asians, especially in the eyes of non-Asians, was the single most obvious feature of similarity, though its significance was differently interpreted.

Some Punjabis distinguished themselves from other Asians by reference to their Sikh religion. One first generation woman, for example, argued that:

> *Only Sikhism recognises the fundamental principle of equality between men and women. For example, all eat together at langar [free communal meals served at gurudwaras, Sikh temples], where men and women of all castes serve other men and women of all castes.*

She contrasted this example of sexual equality with Muslim practice when only men are in charge of mosques and communal affairs; and she contrasted the caste equality with Hinduism in which untouchables and lower castes may not worship or eat together with higher caste Hindus. She also, however, had a strong sense of identity with India, and it was therefore only with non-Indian Asians that she felt she shared nothing positive in common. Other Sikhs of both generations felt decidedly closer to Hindus than to Muslims. One said this was 'because Sikh faith is derived from Hinduism and we are the same people'. Another took this point further and said 'Hindus and Sikhs have similar caste systems'. At the same time, however, they recognised cultural similarities with Muslims, for example with Pakistanis in terms of female dress and a similar Urdu-Hindi derived language which enabled them to enjoy the same films and music. In connection specifically with Muslims a first generation man went even further in stressing commonality.

> *Religion is the only difference. They believe in Islam, we in the ten Gurus and Sikhism. No other differences. Our cultures are the same. We live our lives in the same way, eat the same type of food, have a life with our families which is close.*

A second generation Sikh woman, while again stressing the centrality of sexual equality for Sikhs, also had a strong sense of cultural similarities with other Asians.

In my culture and in my religion, women are perceived as equal to men, if not higher than men. They are encouraged to get an education, encouraged to be independent. This is something I haven't seen from my own experience with Muslims.

The same woman also thought there was an important common feature in South Asian cultures: 'the support that the family and the community give to each other'.

Gujarati Hindus reflected a similar mix and range of views.

There is a great deal of difference between a Gujarati and, say, a Punjabi. Their clothing is more expensive. They wear more jewellery. I cannot find many similarities between our cultures.

Others emphasised difference in diet and dress, as well as language and religion. Yet, while there was less mention of sexual equality and more reference to one's caste (usually to point it out and then say that it was not very important in a British context), there was a sense that, while some Sikhs shared practices and customs with Hindus, non-Gujarati Muslims and Gujarati Hindus were characterised more by differences than similarities. One first generation woman, however, found she had so little in common with non-Gujarati Asians that she found it easier to mix with white people.

Most Pakistanis picked out religion as being central to Pakistanis and so as the most important criterion to judge whether other (Asian) groups were similar to or different from them. Beyond this there was the same spread of views as with the Punjabi Sikhs, and references to the same cultural features (languages, food, dress, family structure and so on). The views of the Bangladeshis mirrored those of the Pakistanis. Islam was seen as the principal basis of similarity with other groups. Some Bangladeshis therefore held the view that there were no cultural similarities with any other Asians except Pakistanis; while the majority, especially among the second generation, were of the view that there were similarities with other Asians but especially so with Pakistanis. Bangladeshis, of all Asian groups, have had the shortest period of residence in Britain. This was reflected in the remarks of two second generation individuals about other Asians. Asked what if any were the differences between Bangladeshis and Pakistanis, one second generation man replied that the former were more committed to 'traditional values' whereas the Pakistanis:

...are less strict about arranged marriages, since being in England longer; more advanced socially and culturally; more advanced educationally, adapted quicker.

Another second generation man drew a similar contrast, adding that Pakistanis had set up more businesses while the older Bangladeshis still think (falsely in his view) 'won't stay here', meaning that they are still caught up in the mentality of an early phase of migration that has been called 'the myth of return' – the idea that the migration is temporary. What was clear was that the main point of reference and comparison for Bangladeshis was Pakistanis, who were viewed positively and as an example to emulate.

One of the consequences of asking Asian respondents to think about similarities to and differences from other Asian groups was that it led some to question whether Asian was a meaningful identity for them. Of those who did choose to comment (less than half the sample), some were negatively inclined towards such an identity but many more, especially among the second generation, were positive, and about the same proportion accepted it purely as a description, including one they would use of themselves, but not as a positive identity. Thus, while those for whom Asian was a positive identity were a minority, those who rejected the idea were few and most used the term to describe themselves and their community. Those who thought of themselves as 'Asians' felt that Asians had much in common, were treated similarly in British society and ought not to let their differences divide them. The main complaint against 'Asian' was that it was an outsider's term and was an excuse for not trying to understand and engage with different Asian groups. Some of those who took pride in their distinctive community identity and traditions felt therefore snubbed by what they saw as the over-use of the term 'Asian' by non-Asians. They said such things as 'white people lump us all together' and 'whites see all brown-skinned people as Asian and don't recognise differences between different Asian communities'. A second generation Punjabi man spoke for many when he said 'whites who are racist see me as a "Paki", others that don't know me see me as an "Asian"'.

Some of those who embraced an Asian identity felt it was a natural development as the distinctive Asian cultures became diluted in Britain over time, adapted to British society and began to resemble each other more. Thus a second generation Gujarati woman said:

I would prefer to be called an Asian rather than be segregated into castes. I am an Asian first, then Gujarati.

Similarly, a second generation Pakistani woman said:

So many of my friends do not identify themselves as Pakistanis or call themselves 'Pakistanis', do not speak the language or know anything about the country. They don't go to Pakistan on visits. They don't identify Pakistan as their home.

She therefore felt that the main issue was whether Asians in Britain were to have any Asian identity at all and not whether that it should be, say,

Pakistani or Bangladeshi. Some of those who wanted to have a positive Asian identity felt constrained by stereotypes about Asians. One Punjabi second generation woman resented being seen as 'a submissive Asian woman', just because she wore traditional dress and did not believe in dating, while another felt uncomfortable that because she lived on her own and did not wear traditional dress white people tended to discount her Asianness.

Some, however, felt that there was no such thing as an Asian identity. A Pakistani second generation man argued:

> *The term 'Asian' is artificial; it doesn't account for differences. It's too wide to have any meaning. It is simply a colour, because all Asians are a similar colour. But colour is not a good reflection to identify oneself.*

While several people pointed to the common physical appearance, as an obvious point of similarity between Asians, most of them did not share the view that there were not other commonalities or that Asian could not be a positive identity. Others who rejected an Asian identity did so not because it focused on colour or diminished a sub-Asian identity but because it was eclipsed by a broader and more important identity. Several second generation respondents, particularly among the Punjabis, thought that a focus on colour was instructive because it made plain that Asianness was constructed by white people to designate a racial group, an 'Other'. It therefore highlighted the background of racism in which debates about ethnic identity took place and the importance of racism, rather than minority cultures, in shaping the lives of Asian people. For these respondents the term 'Asian' signified that the individuals so-called suffered from a common experience of racism; but so did other individuals, most notably Afro-Caribbeans. Hence the important anti-racist colour-identity was not 'brown' or 'Asian' but 'black', for that enabled a broader unity and a more effective political challenge to racism.

> *The issue of racism is very important in how I see myself. I identify with 'black' as a political term because, to fight racism effectively, minority groups need to be united. Calling yourself different ethnic groups in the battle against racism is divisive and ineffective.*

Some of the six people who held this view had many Caribbean friends and felt culturally close to them.

> *Obviously we originate from different continents and maybe in my parents' time our ways of life were very different. I feel that today I have a lot in common with them in terms of social life, music – for example, I love black American music, soul, rhythm and blues and music like that.*

This perception of a shared culture, usually multi-racial rather than just black-Asian, centring on music, 'going-out', dress and so on, existed too among some second generation people who did not necessarily espouse a 'black' political identity. On the other hand, it was a minority view. While most of the Asian respondents recognised that the Caribbeans were, like themselves, 'foreigners', 'immigrants', 'minorities' and 'suffer-the-same-racism', most said that there were little or no cultural similarities between their own group and Afro-Caribbeans.

This was very clearly the predominant view amongst the first generation people, some of whom also expressed negative views about Caribbeans, and the list of dissimilarities included reference to religion, language, family structure, marriages, dress and food. Most who held this view also said that Caribbeans had been able to adapt to and integrate into British life much more easily, and some took this to the extreme arguing that there was no real cultural difference between whites and blacks.

The second generation was more divided on the question but the majority thought there were little or no cultural similarity between their community and the Caribbeans. Of all second generation Asians, the Bangladeshis most consistently took this view, yet the common experience of racism could override differences in cultural background, as with one woman who argued both that, compared to that of the Bangladeshis, the Afro-Caribbean 'life-style is different ... lots of differences' and that she felt 'part of the black community, more comfortable, more secure than when mixing with white people'. In contrast, a second generation Gujarati woman said she had 'more in common with white British people than blacks'. At least one of those who gave priority to the common experience of racism went on to emphasise that racism affected different groups differently.

> *The experience of being a minority and suffering racism is different. For example, they were slaves, we were colonised; they are labelled as trouble makers and criminals, we Asians labelled as hard-working shopkeepers – both myths.*

Yet if different groups are seen as in some ways moving closer to each other, this was not necessarily to be welcomed. A second generation Bangladeshi man expressed concern that young Bangladeshis were following young Caribbean men in getting increasingly involved in drugs, criminal activity and violence.

South Asian perceptions of 'Britishness'
Some Asians responded to the questions about Britishness by saying that theoretically everyone with British citizenship, regardless of colour and

origins, was equally British. For example, a Gujarati woman who came to Britain in the 1960s, when she was already in her mid-forties (and who had earlier in the interview stated 'I see no difference in the way that I live today and the way my mother lived'), said: 'In my opinion a British person is a person who is a British subject, or is born in Britain.' But she went on to say why she believed this did not work in practice:

There should not be any discrimination between blacks and whites as far as being British is concerned, but I have noticed that there is a 'colour-bar' in operation in that white people may lessen our Britishness.

In denying that 'Britishness' had any cultural content she took her view to its logical conclusion:

I do not think that my children are more British than I am. There is no behavioral or cultural uniqueness in being British. You don't have to be modern or outgoing to be British.

Racism in the attitude of white people to ethnic minorities was identified by many as being critical to whether they would, regardless of formal citizenship or birth in Britain, think of themselves as British. We did not explicitly ask questions about racism, as opposed to barriers to feeling British, except in one respect: we asked whether people had experienced any racial violence or harassment in the last twelve months. The levels reported by the South Asians were high: 20 out of the 49 Asians (40 per cent) had a personal experience including seven of physical attack (14 per cent). The Punjabis and the Bangladeshis had higher rates of victimisation than the Gujaratis and the Pakistanis, a variation which could partly be the result of where our respondents came from (see Table 1 in Chapter 1).

One of the consequences of this level of violence and harassment was that people made changes to how they lived, though fear of attack was as strong a factor as recent personal experience. Nearly half of all Asians said that experience or fear of racial victimisation had made them modify their behaviour, mainly in not going out to certain places of entertainment (especially pubs) or to certain 'white areas' at night, or to not going out at all at night.

Most of the first generation of South Asians neither said they were 'British' nor wanted to be. They had a strong sense of their own cultural difference, of the difference between the society in which they were brought up and still connected to, and the one they had settled in:

Bangladeshi living style is very different from British living style. Here everyone lives for themselves, individual lives, no sense of community (Bangladeshi man).

There is a lot of difference. Our cultures differ – obviously no matter if the Asian has lived in the UK 25 years or 30 years. There are differences in our cultures, white people have a separate unique culture from our own. They are more 'British' than an Asian ever could be (Gujarati woman).

British? No, I feel Indian because I was born in India and my heart lies in India because that's where I grew up. I can't forget where I was born and raised (Sikh woman).

Not us, however long we stay – we are Pakistanis living in Britain. People who feel love for the country are 'really' British (Pakistani woman).

But such first generation respondents recognised that their children, schooled and socialised in Britain, were more British than themselves. They found it difficult, however, to offer an alternative to the 'essential difference' model or to explain in what ways their children were (for example) Punjabi and not British, and vice versa.

Other first generation respondents, especially among the men and among Pakistanis, took a less 'either-or' view about themselves. They felt that the attempts that they had made and were making to adapt to British life did indeed mean that they were British in some sense more than mere formal citizenship.

Being 'British' means living in British society and living as a British citizen, of 'when in Rome do as the Romans do', of being faithful to the country while of course keeping one's own culture.

Such people spoke of the need to 'integrate' and 'adapt' but emphasised also the importance of retaining one's ethnic and religious identity and of bringing up their children accordingly. They were confident that Asians were British, though they felt that white people needed to overcome their racist intolerance of other cultures, and that everybody needed to practice 'mutual respect for other other's values'.

The main division, then, among the first generation on their relationship to British society was between the majority who thought of themselves as hard-working, law-abiding, tax-paying citizens at peace with the wider society but culturally distinct from it; and those, more often male and more educated, who saw their citizenship as implying an active interest in British institutions and society, adopting British ways and mixing with all kinds of Britons socially, whilst still holding on to their ethnic identity in a bi-cultural way.

As might be expected, the debate about Britishness takes a different form among the second generation, though again these two views predominate. Some second generation respondents argued for a more developed version of the bi-cultural view but felt more acutely than the first generation that cultural difference is not accepted by white British people, so that there was continual social pressure to minimise one's ethnic identity. More than half of the second generation said they felt culturally British to a large extent and evidenced their appearance, forms of socialising, choice of entertainment among other features, but also felt strongly that they were still not accepted by white people as British and so could not call themselves 'British'.

In this way, both of these groups, comprising nearly all the second generation sample, identified majority racism as the main issue. By thinking of Britishness exclusively in terms of 'whiteness' (regardless of the legal position or political declarations), white people made it difficult if not impossible for Asians (and Afro-Caribbeans) to identify with Britain in a positive way. Additionally, a minority of the second generation said they felt alienated from a British culture which seemed no longer interested in moral values centred on family, religion and community.

Second generation respondents who felt largely culturally British came from each of the South Asian groups, but they were particularly strongly represented among the Punjabis.

Culturally in terms of how I live my life, for example, arts, cinema, clubs, music, I have lots in common with white British or parts of them. It would be surprising if I didn't. Being born here, I went to the same schools, took same exams, same universities, have mixed friends, it would be very surprising if I had remained like my parents, that's to say, culturally Indian. They were immigrants, weren't educated here, and the only friends they had at first were Indian because no one else would talk to them. I was born in Britain, I hold a British passport, am culturally British and yet I still don't believe or feel or describe myself as British, because in general whites look at my brown skin-colour and think to themselves 'foreigner'. They have not understood or cannot understand that brown people can be British, are just as British as them. Until they change their attitudes, I will never be able to honestly say I am British (Punjabi professional man).

Similarly, a Punjabi woman who said that in terms of education, career aspirations and socialising, her life was similar to that of her white friends, nevertheless felt that 'being British doesn't mean anything to me' and asked 'because of racism, how can I say this is my country?'. She explained that Indians suffered from this racism because 'we don't look like white English people and we live differently from them in certain ways'.

Those who felt that they themselves were culturally mixed believed that it was a positive feature about themselves, that it was not incompatible with being British except that the 'arrogant cultural narrow-mindedness' of white people made it so. In a group discussion it was argued that 'many Asians have a conflict: we have a strong pull to our culture but also we are getting the best out of living in Britain'. This potential tension was thought by some to be capable of resolution; several spoke of 'trying to take the best from both worlds and marrying them together'. One example given was of a practising Hindu woman who was 'traditional' as regards family ethics but 'modern' in terms of educational and career aspirations. A woman who called herself 'British Pakistani' and defined this as 'having a background more than basic British' emphasised the importance of being 'flexible' and 'adjusting yourself' to different groups and changing circumstances. She identified attitudes to 'skin colour, different cultures and not integrating' as 'barriers to being British'.

Several others described themselves in hyphenated terms like 'some Gujarati but also some English' or 'British-Bengali'. They were usually positive about being British and using the term 'British' of themselves, but they were concerned to retain significant elements of their family upbringing or ethnic or religious identity. They were, much more than the first generation, conscious of the difficulties of this. While some thought that parents not allowing their children enough of an ethnically-mixed social life was a problem, most put the blame on a racism-cum-cultural intolerance on the part of the majority of white people. They argued that the majoritarian view was that 'to be British you have to give up your own culture'. This, they thought, was an unreasonable demand that must be opposed.

> We shouldn't have to be accepted by the British. If they have a problem with that, then it makes them ignorant.

Finally, there were a few second generation Asians who rejected 'being British' not just because of racist exclusion but because they were in ethical opposition to aspects of British society most visible to them.

> Indian, because British don't make me feel at home. I don't feel at home with them or their ethics. Their way of life is largely alien compared to mine. That's all in the definition of being Indian (young Sikh woman).

Similarly, a Pakistani man thought that western ways of living were too individualistic for Asians in general, and that for Muslims a barrier to being British was that British culture was too secular for them to feel comfortable in. (Interestingly, one of the similarities between Pakistanis and British in his opinion was a 'stiff upper lip'.)

Comment

A broadening of ethnic identities has clearly been taking place. This is evident in the choice of labels that respondents felt were most appropriate in most contexts in Britain: in the movement from describing oneself in terms of the island of origin to a pan-Caribbean identification or black; and from caste identification to Hindu and Sikh or to Indian or Asian. Yet there is at the same time a strong sense of ethnic and religious distinctiveness vis-à-vis not just the white British but also other non-white minorities. Some forms of self-definition identifying micro-ethnicities or distinctions that cut no ice outside an ethnic group dissolve or coalesce into more viable groupings, at least at the level of public discourse. Nevertheless the broadening of identities is premised upon a perception of commonality – a commonality based for the most part on regional, national or continental origins and heritage (for example, Gujarati, Indian and African), or on historical divisions, religion or physical appearance (black, Asian), rather than on some generalised status derived from how these groups are treated by the British majority (immigrant, ethnic minority, political blackness). The point of reference is origins rather than a new identity that transcends or transmutes ethnicity, as expressed, for example, in the ideas of political blackness or Islamism. These ideas are present in some ethnic minority discourses, and for some people are a greater, more principled basis for social identity than merely ethnic origins, but for most of our respondents the primary minority identification refers to a place or a distinctive way of living, to a symbolic link with a people outside Britain.

Of course, some people wanted explicitly to declare a link with Britain too and this was most evident in the hyphenated description of themselves such as British-Pakistani and in their suggestions that they had a mixed identity because of the different influences upon their lives. It is also likely that our respondents had other personal and social identities that were important to them in many contexts, perhaps for some more important than an ethnic minority identity. These identities could relate to gender, class, occupation, locality, political beliefs, popular culture, sport and so on, any of which can be of more importance than ethnicity in terms of self-definition and behaviour. In this study we confined our attention to respondents' descriptions of their ethnic identity and while we inquired what they thought they had in common with others outside their group, we did not investigate their non-ethnic identities.

The most successful example of the broadening of ethnic identities is that of pan-Caribbean identity in Britain, (on the prevalence of island identities at the time of migration and for some time later see Pollard, 1972; Brooks, 1975:312-14; Midgett, 1975; Western, 1992), a success which cannot simply be measured in terms of how many respondents used the term 'Caribbean' in their primary description of themselves. While a significant number of respondents used that term (or 'West Indian', as the first generation marginally preferred), the predominant identity amongst the group was black. Yet it was clear from what respondents said that Caribbean, black, black-Caribbean, black-British were used interchangeably; many respondents felt that the terms were synonyms, different attempts to describe the same group identity. The different terms were not only perceived to be not in competition with each other (which would be true if they marked different but compatible identities like black and woman) but, more importantly, to be describing the same ethnicity.

The crucial point is that, regardless of the choice of label, the Caribbean-origin respondents saw themselves as members of the same group. It is interesting to note that some came to have a stronger sense of Caribbean identity as a result of being thought of as English when visiting the island of their origins. It had the effect of leading them to give up an island identity (for example, Antiguan) but it did not necessarily make them feel British, because it did not deal with the problem of non-acceptance by the white British. There was a break with the past but the compensatory new 'belonging' in the present was not with British society as such but with those of Caribbean origins in Britain and perhaps elsewhere (James, 1993).

Such an identity formation can be understood only in the context of the development of black consciousness in the last few decades amongst the descendants of Africans in the United States, Britain and elsewhere in the context of struggles against racism. There was, however, relatively little espousal of an 'African' identity, unlike in the United States, where 'African-American' is largely replacing 'black' in public discourse.

Regardless of the choice of terms, the taken-for-granted existence of a British pan-Caribbean identity comes out most clearly when it is contrasted to a British pan-South Asian identity. There was certainly some identification, especially among second generation South Asians, with the term Asian, but it was more passive than active and secondary to a more specific ethnic or religious identity. Most importantly, some Asians, including some from the second generation, questioned whether there was enough commonality to sustain an Asian identity which was more than simply a racial identity of 'brown' or 'Paki' and some assorted stereotypes. In line with this many Asians believed that there were significant cultural, linguistic, religious and national-origin differences between Asians, though two coalitions were evident, one around Indian and the other around Muslim.

The problems, then, that beset a pan-Asian identity were not paralleled in the pan-Caribbean case. Caribbean respondents did not question the existence of a distinctive Caribbean grouping (regardless of whether group unity was evident in terms of action). They did not claim that this identity was secondary to some sub-grouping or groupings based on religion or language or island-origins with a greater claim upon their consciousness and was an obstacle to Caribbean unity. Above all, they had turned a racial description of themselves, based on their physical appearance, into a positive term of self-identification, black; whereas for most Asians their sense of a racial identity was relatively weak compared to an ethnic or religious identity (Modood, 1990).

Most of the Asians who said that racism was a major factor in shaping their minority condition were not enthusiastic about a positive Asian identity. For them the logic of an opposition to a white racism against non-white people was to develop an inclusive non-white identity. As this was the rationale behind the emergence of a 'black' political identity, it was this identity that they wanted to combine with their own ethnic identity, leaving no special role for a pan-South Asian identity. As those who espoused a 'black' identity were mainly among those second generation respondents who said they thought of themselves as culturally British, for whom religion was not important and who had a social life based around ethnically-mixed friendships and mainstream youth culture, it may be thought that as such a grouping is bound to grow, so too will Asian involvement in 'black' identity.

This common-sense prediction cannot be dismissed but it does need to be balanced against three other considerations. First, not only do South Asians at the moment have a weak identification with the anti-racist concept of blackness, but in fact it may be the case that the concept is in decline. From the 1970s onwards sociologists, political activists and local authorities began to use a discourse of blackness to describe South Asians as well as Caribbeans, arguing that this was how these groups conceived of themselves once they grasped the imperatives of anti-racism (Modood, 1994b). In the last few years, however, some sociologists have come to argue that that phase of anti-racism is over, that blackness no longer enjoys a 'hegemony' over ethnic minorities and the relevant discourses (Modood, 1988; Hall, 1992; Ali, 1991; Anthias and Yuval-Davis, 1992; Bonnett, 1993; Gillborn, 1995). Perhaps a good illustration of the rise and decline of the inclusive category of 'black' is its standing with the Commission for Racial Equality (CRE). In 1982, the then Chairman of the CRE told the House of Commons Home Affairs sub-committee that despite the fact that the majority of Asians would not self-classify themselves as 'black', this was 'the conventional way now of regarding all those who suffer from the particular disadvantage related to colour' (House of Commons, 1982: para 391). In 1988, however, the CRE withdrew its recommendation that Asians should be classified as 'black' for the purposes of ethnic monitoring (CRE, 1988).

Secondly, going beyond the languages of official and political discourse, it is not at all clear that there was ever a time when at a grass-roots level many Asians identified with 'black'. Anecdotal reports suggest that this may have happened within some localised communities at a time of severe racism, for example in Southall in the late 1970s, but there is no evidence that support was more widespread. The only real measure of Asian opinion on this matter comes from a BBC viewers' poll. The BBC Asian television programme *Network East,* the audience of which is weighted towards the second generation, carried an item on this issue in March 1989. Despite several speakers accusing Asians who objected to being called 'black' of being racist, stupid and divisive, nearly two-thirds of the over 3,000 who took part in the subsequent telephone poll rejected the term 'black' for Asians. More solid data will be available from the Fourth National Survey.

Thirdly, political blackness is not just a matter of anti-racism; its success is bound to depend upon the extent to which the various non-white groups find bases of relationship in addition to being victims of racism. As has already been discussed, there is only a limited sense of Asianness amongst the South Asian groups. Our fieldwork also shows that there is weak mutual identification and perception of similarities between Asians and Caribbeans. The majority of each group believes that they are culturally dissimilar to each other, that the Caribbeans share a common culture with the white British but that the Asians are different, being organised as religious communities and less interested in integrating with British society. There is some support for the idea of a common thread woven out of oppression in the British Empire, the experience of migration to Britain and contemporary racism; but each group also has negative images of the other (see also James, 1993:267-70). There is some evidence of less distance among members of the second generation but it does not yet seem to amount to a special relationship. Indeed, the discussions about friendship and the choice of marriage partners suggest that most Asians are outside the relationship that Caribbeans and whites are evolving together.

It is, however, true that the perception of racism is for South Asians and for Caribbeans critical to their alienation from 'being British' and to their sense of their ethnicity. For many Caribbeans and for second generation Asians the sense of exclusion by white people is one of the principal reinforcements of their sense of ethnic identity. It is important, however, to note that the perceived racism in question is a complex racism and can affect different groups differently.

Racial violence and harassment give the clearest and the most extreme case of rejection, of not being accepted as British. Other research is in line with the findings from our small samples that racial harassment is more common against Asians than Caribbeans. Our study also shows that Asian communities are generally more inward-looking and encapsulated, and it is likely that harassment has contributed to or prolonged this process. It may well be that the perceived cultural difference of Asians attracts racist hostility. If this is so, Asian withdrawal, by way of defence, into their own communities, and Asian use of their ethnicity to assert their rights, may in turn isolate them further and heighten the hostility against them.

The important point is that the increase in public assertions of ethnicity and of political demands associated with ethnicity in the last few years, what in the Introduction we called 'public ethnicity', often in the form of a defensive cultural or religious conservatism (Modood, 1990 and 1992), is related to the experience of exclusion and harassment. What may on the surface appear to be merely a minority religious revivalism or a natural development of a South Asian cultural practice may in fact be caused partly by hostile elements in the dominant society. In conditions of insecurity it is not surprising if individuals and communities cling to and assert what gives them psychological strength. These forms of insecure assertiveness can raise the political profile of the minority or minorities in question. But it can itself lead to increased majority hostility and stimulate more rejectionism. On the other hand the Caribbean example illustrates that an initial desire to affirm membership of the majority culture is far from guaranteed a positive majority response. In this respect Michael Banton has perhaps well captured how white majority opinion can shift from one view of 'integration ' to another. He has argued that in the early years of ex-empire immigration:

> The English seemed to display more hostility towards the West Indians because they sought a greater degree of acceptance than the English wished to accord; in more recent times there seems to have been more hostility towards Asians because they are insufficiently inclined to adopt English ways (Banton, 1979: 242).

A harassed minority is thus caught in a fork: attempts to join the mainstream no less than assertions of distinctiveness and ethnic pride can stimulate racial hostility including harassment and violence. Either way, the fate of the minority depends upon the attitudes of the majority.

Many respondents were acutely aware that whether there was overt hostility or not, they were all too often constrained by or had to overcome negative stereotypes about their ethnic group. Some Caribbean respondents pointed to stereotypes of Caribbeans that haunt even the closest of black-white relationships and some pointed to how the media, by acts of commission and omission, reinforce these stereotypes. Similarly, Asians complained about stereotypes about Asians or 'Pakis'. They also mentioned, in particular, the oppressive stereotypes about 'the Asian woman' and 'Muslim fundamentalists'. Some respondents clearly felt they were being asked to mute or eliminate their cultural identity in order to have a chance of social acceptance and equal rights with the white British. The racism, then, that was perceived as the main barrier to Britishness, especially by some of the Asians, is a complex of what can be called colour-racism and cultural-racism (Modood, 1994).

What is perhaps true in the suggestion that a 'black' identity could become important to Asians as their sense of cultural difference fades is that minority identities seem to be increasingly shaped by a sense of exclusion. This sense of exclusion is by no means simply focused on colour, but it does seem that the more 'acculturated' a non-white group or individual is, that is to say the more culturally British, the greater their sense of racial or colour-based exclusion. On the one hand, the fact of cultural commonality makes plain to individuals that race or colour must be the ground of exclusion since there are no other bases for it. On the other hand, a strong sense of socio-cultural identification with the majority and a racially mixed social life can create greater sensitivity to the process of exclusion and put one in more situations where it takes place. Groups whose personal and social lives are more centred on their minority communities may, unless they are actively victimised, be more immune to, and more ignorant of, what the majority think of them, and may be more likely to seek an acceptance of their difference and hope for peaceful co-existence.

Hence, while most second generation Caribbeans seem to take their Britishness as a fact and emphasise their colour-exclusion as the obstacle to their being accepted as British, some second generation Asians seem to feel their Britishness is more precarious or is dependent on their giving up their parental culture; for them, a hyphenated identity, the simultaneous affirmation of their Britishness and their ethnicity, is therefore spoken of as something positive and a basis for mutual accommodation. For those who feel that culturally they are similar to their white peers and have an awareness that they are treated less favourably than their white peers, the question of cultural negotiation and mutual accommodation does not arise. As they do not consider that they or their group are making any special cultural demands upon the socio-political system, for them the issues reduce themselves to colour-racism.

However, even among acculturated individuals more than one response to colour-exclusion is possible and can be found amongst our respondents. One form of response is for individuals to assert the identity of their upbringing or some variation of it, such as Gujarati-Indian, Afro-Caribbean or Muslim. People thus seek some psychological security in affirming an alternative identity to the one they are being excluded from, and a solidarity with a culture or community that they know something of and that is part of their biography, even if it is not an accurate description of their current way of living. This surely is the situation of those second generation Asians who describe themselves as mainly culturally British but who do not think of themselves in terms of a colour-identity or, in so far as they do, think of themselves in terms of 'Asian', a term which combines a colour (brown) and a cultural reference. For them the negative fact of a colour-exclusion gives rise not to a corresponding positive colour-identity but to a desire for ethnic pride, a desire to stand by one's ethnic origins. It is, in the terms used in the Introduction, an assertive strategy based on the symbolic power of a mode of being.

The alternative response is to seek an identity that reflects the common feature of the various kinds of racial exclusions; to seek strength not from one's family's heritage but from the history and politics of opposition to racism. These two responses, an ethnic affirmation and a political blackness, are not necessarily incompatible. This can be seen in how some Caribbeans use the concept of 'black' to refer to and synthesise a specific cultural community and a heritage of racist suffering and anti-racist opposition. Yet this synthesis gives political 'black' an Afrocentric bias, producing a concept which is difficult to import with South Asian heritages and values (Bonnett, 1993:44). For Caribbeans 'black' (when not just an external attribute) is an ethnic heritage or a political identity, or ideally both; for South Asians 'black' is at best a political identity that is neutral in terms of their cultural heritage and religion. Hence the use of 'black' which aims to combine the two assertive strategies rests on an internal tension: politically, it reaches out to Asians but is grounded on a celebration of African-Caribbean roots.

The process influencing group identity can be complex. A group which opposes racial exclusion by emphasising its lack of difference from the white majority may well, in the face of continuing racism, be led to mobilise opposition and generate group self-confidence and thus consciously seek to develop and emphasise a culturally distinctive identity. An example of this process is the case of the Caribbeans. While most Caribbeans affirm a cultural commonality with the white British, we have seen that some have been led, through a process of countering exclusion, to emphasise a distinct cultural identity. We have also seen that, while the first generation are inclined to emphasise the Britishness of their children, there is an interest in ethnic renewal amongst the second generation, especially in distinctive languages (and literature, poetry and music, which we have not considered in this study). Thus the two strategies of ethnic assertiveness and political blackness can be either supplementary or competitive, a critical determinant being how much cultural content is conferred upon blackness. The more that 'blackness' stands for a renewal of a Caribbean or ancestral African ethnicity, the less its scope as an ethnically-neutral basis for uniting the victims of racism.

It is equally important to note that these two assertive strategies do not imply (though in their extreme versions they can lead to) a rejection of 'British', to an ethnic or racial separation. Rather, they are a search for dignity and a rejection of inequality. They are in effect a rejection of the view of minorities as petitioners asking to be let into a white society which they hold to be the source of all value, of minorities as having no worth except that which white people are willing to assign them. By asserting a valued non-white identity and demanding some respect for it, minorities seek to bestow some status upon themselves. This assertion may sometimes be only at a political or public discourse level, rather than in terms of cultural practices at the level of daily life. Yet the negotiation for social and political inclusion then becomes less of a one-way affair, for the excluded can present themselves in a more positive light and build an insurance policy against further exclusion. It may seem contradictory for people to emphasise the importance of their ethnic heritage to them and to say at the same time that they see themselves as mainly culturally British. Different people mean somewhat different things by this combination, but the common ground is an objection to the racist arrogance implicit in assimilationism.

Most of the second generation (and some of the first generation) do indeed identify with important aspects of British society – even while often rejecting the possibility of being British, or more precisely, of being accepted as British. This is because in practice they identify with and actively participate in important features of British society while reserving the terms 'British' for those features with which they do not identify or feel they are not allowed to identify with. This can be brought out if we divide

'Britishness' into three components: the historical legacy, opportunities in education and work, and social life.

Historical legacy

This is usually described by the interviewees as white, nostalgic about Empire, xenophobic, racist and (by Asians) Christian. Historical Britain is largely seen negatively, perhaps even stereotypically, indeed as 'the problem'. This view, while predominant, is not unanimous. For example, some Pakistanis and Bangladeshis mentioned ancestral connection with a country as the basis of 'true' belonging. A female Gujarati student, fluent in three Indian languages, described herself as 'British Indian ... I have gained so much from the British culture that to say I was just Indian would not be representative of who I am'. But she identified 'a sense of history' as a barrier to being British:

> *My sense of history in this country isn't as strong as people who are 'pure' British, people who have lived here for generations and have a proud sense of identity which I don't have.*

Most second generation respondents, however, made no mention of the possibility of a positive British heritage. This was in striking contrast to their declarations about the importance of their own ancestry and heritage, about 'knowing where you are coming from' and 'being in touch with your history, your roots'. Despite or perhaps because of their own concern with an extra-British heritage and roots, they showed little appreciation of Britain as roots. It would probably be fair to say that for most of them any explicit talk of pride in British roots by white British people rings alarm bells about white supremacy and imperial domination.

Education and work opportunities

This is the one area about which all speak positively and compare favourably with the country of their origins. It is a reason often given by first generation respondents as the advantage of being in Britain, especially for their children, and by second generation respondents as the basis of commonality with whites, despite their also frequently mentioning the persistence of a racial discrimination that prevented them from competing with their white peers.

Social life

This is the main area of division between the respondents. Most Caribbeans had no special view about British social life, which they felt they in the main shared except for being marginalised or discriminated against. Other

Caribbean respondents felt they had to mute their 'blackness' in order to be acceptable in certain white circles; others again enjoyed a multi-ethnic social life and friendships and shared black music and culture with other British people. A few Caribbean respondents felt the need to withdraw from British culture in order to rediscover their distinctive heritage.

Similarly, perhaps even more so, social life is a dimension which divided the Asians, especially between the generations, in terms of how 'British' Asians should be. Many young Asians thought there was little or no difference between their social life and that of their white and black peers. Indeed, some thought that this was the essence of Britishness. A Bangladeshi man said:

> *Being British? Live life, go to discos, nightclubs, pizza restaurants, keeping up with fashions, seeing latest pictures...*

Yet, as we have seen from this and earlier chapters, this was the kind of social life that much of the first generation did not want their children to be part of, and which some second generation individuals felt alienated from. Such second generation respondents were in a minority but their outlook might become more widely shared as their generation marries, has children and comes to play a bigger role in family and community affairs. Most of the Asian second generation wanted to retain some core heritage, some amalgam of family cohesion, religion and language, probably in an adapted form, but did not expect this to mean segregated social lives, for they lived and wanted to live in an ethnically mixed way.

7 Conclusion

> A white Briton who does not understand the cultural accents of
> his Muslim or Afro-Caribbean fellow-citizens is just as
> incompletely British as the Indian ignorant of the ways his white
> fellow citizens speak. In other words none of us *is* fully British.
> We are all constantly trying to *become* one, each in his own way
> and at his own pace. Only he is fully British who can honestly
> say that no British citizen, black or white, Christian or Hindu, is
> a cultural stranger to him. Those generally regarded as
> quintessentially British are in some ways the least British.
> (Bhikhu Parekh, 1990:75)

We sought, through interviews and group discussions with 74 people,
to build an understanding of what their ethnic background means to
members of the main minority groups. For the South Asians, the two
variables were national/regional origins and religion. With the Caribbeans,
they were regional origins and African descent. Additionally, the study was
structured so that we could compare the migrant with the British-born
generation and focus on the changes that have been and are taking place in
the various ethnic identities, especially in how they relate to conceptions of
Britishness.

Family and social contacts
We found that family structures have undergone considerable change from
the pre-migration period. The extended family networks of the Caribbeans
have not been carried over to Britain and there is no longer a collective
solving of child-care and financial problems within the wider family or the
wider community. Half of the Caribbean respondents were in regular
contact only with immediate family members. There was a strong feeling
of mutual obligations, however, within the immediate family, but here too
change was evident. The first generation felt that their children, growing
up in Britain, did not give them the automatic respect *they* had given to their
own parents. Parents had, in the main, adapted to this generational change
and had come to have, with their children, more of a relationship between

equals with advice and support flowing in both directions. Feelings of financial independence were present in both generations.

Between the two Caribbean generations the church has declined in favour of education and work as the place where friendships are made and sustained. Most Caribbean respondents had friends from other ethnic groups, though half of the first generation and a third of the second generation had only other Caribbeans as close friends. In both generations friends were chosen on the basis of shared experience, real or imagined, including that of ethnicity. Moreover, the experience of racism was often extremely important to the second generation in choosing friends. There was little if any difference in the type of activities shared between family members and friends regardless of ethnicity. Caribbeans were, on the whole, not committed to an ethnic preference in any absolute sense in the context of giving or receiving help but some respondents felt that the inadequacy of existing mainstream services in meeting the needs of Caribbean people had left them with no option but an ethnic group basis for self-help and voluntary community work. Some of those who were active in organisations set up specifically for Caribbean people saw their work as contributing also to the wider goals of black cultural pride and black unity.

For the first generation South Asians the extended family was an important institution of mutual support and transmission of values, and the main sphere of social life. Members of an extended family had high levels of contact with each other, seeing at least some other members once or twice a week, and would expect to give financial assistance to each other, including sending money 'back home'. If social life extended beyond the extended family it was within the ethno-religious community and was likely to be focused around a local temple or mosque. The absence of friends outside their own community was explained by first generation respondents by reference to language and the importance of shared values and norms as a basis for friendship; some respondents were also discomforted that a lot of socialising in Britain involved the imbibing of alcohol.

The second generation Asians, however, had much less contact with the extended family which was, at least up to this stage of their lives, hardly conceived of as a support system. Much of the value that the first generation placed on the extended family, the second generation placed instead on the immediate family meaning parents, siblings and probably grandparents. While this probably means that their lives are more centred around the family than their non-Asian peers in Britain, it also means that their social life is unlikely to be centred around the extended family but rather around relationships formed through work or educational institution. Most of this generation, consequently, had friends from outside their ethno-religious communities, particularly if they were or had been in higher education. For most respondents, however, their closest friends were from their own ethnic background or were at least Asian. The reasons given for this were to some extent similar to those of the first generation, namely the importance of similar backgrounds, interests and values; but some mentioned the need for mutual support against racism and cultural isolation, and others that it was a consequence of their ethnic identity.

Community languages

Both the South Asian generations thought it important to maintain the ✗ learning and use of their ethnic group languages. It was generally perceived that the use of these languages was in decline, with increasing numbers of second generation respondents not only unable to read or write in the relevant language but also restricting the spoken language to home and family. But some counter-action was being taken. For example, some communities were organising classes and most Asian respondents wanted Asian languages to be taught in state schools.

The Caribbean first generation on the other hand were relatively unworried by the decline in the use of Patois and Creole. There was, however, a resurgence of interest amongst the second generation in Creole and Patois as part of a new emphasis on cultural identity. The first generation took a predominantly practical approach to language, judging a language by its utility in offering career opportunities. The second generation valued their ancestral languages for putting them in touch with a history, a culture and a part of the world that for some was only ever seen on rare holidays and on television screens.

Religion

For the majority of the first generation Caribbeans and nearly all first λ generation Asians religion was of considerable importance to how they lived their lives. It gave them a moral structure, with its emphasis on familial obligations and opposition to a materialist, hedonist or selfish view of life. The Caribbeans were more likely to emphasise the power of prayer in bringing them close to God, in giving strength to cope with difficulties that arose and in celebrating joyful occasions. Some also spoke of the church as a family group to give and take support from when needed. The Asians were more likely to emphasise the regularity of prayer and attendance at a place of worship and the restrictions on food and drink, though they also spoke of the celebration of holy festivals. For most first generation Asians religion was central to their cultural identity and for some it was of more importance than any other aspect of ethnicity.

Virtually all the first generation respondents had brought their children up within their faith and, while the Asians expected their children to live within it, the Caribbeans hoped they would but expected them to decide for themselves upon reaching adulthood. All the second generation Caribbeans had been brought up as practising Christians but over half felt that religion no longer played an important part in their lives. They viewed religion as a set of behavioural restrictions out of touch with their daily realities. The importance of Christianity for those second generation respondents who were still influenced by it centred on the supportive nature of the church community. They also attributed a sense of stability in their lives to adherence to their faith. It was considered central to educational and career progress because it kept them 'out of trouble' and away from negative influences. While some of the first generation spoke of Christianity as an important part of their cultural heritage and identity, in general the second generation did not. Neither the minority who were practising Christians nor the majority who were not made any special connection between Christianity and their ethnicity.

The Asian second generation too did not give religion the same kind of importance as the Asian first generation. This was particularly so with the Sikhs, only one of whom thought that religion was important. Even she, however, confessed that like the rest of her peer group she did not attend the temple or pray regularly. In fact the young Sikhs attended the temple only when required to do so for a festival or a wedding. Yet, in differing degrees, they held the view that Sikhism was part of their ethnic heritage and they would wish to hand it on to their children.

The second generation Hindus were more likely to say that religion was important in the way they led their life, yet they, too, rarely attended a temple. For them religion was a matter of personal spiritual fulfilment and therefore each individual had to practice it in the way it suited them. Some did however also emphasise the religious basis of their code of behaviour concerning food and drink, dress and socialising, some of them instancing pubs and mini-skirts as things with which they were not comfortable. Even so they tended to observe the Hindu prohibition on beef more than the prohibition on alcohol. Other second generation Hindus, particularly men, frankly admitted that religion was an irrelevance to them and regretted that to please their parents they would have to restrict their choice of marriage partner to Hindus. Yet they were not inclined to deny that Hinduism was part of their cultural heritage and they expected to want to pass it on to their children.

Among the second generation Asians it was the Muslims who spoke most positively about the value and centrality of their religion. Most said that Islam was 'very important' to how they lived their lives. But it was obvious that beyond this emphatic affirmation there were currents of questioning, revision and even a pressured conformity. Nearly all the second generation Muslims said they were not strict in the observance of the various requirements of their faith, and several felt a tension between the demands of their faith and the life they thought appropriate in contemporary England. One of them, encouraged by her father, had gone a long way in re-interpreting Islam as an ethical philosophy without an array of petty rules. Like their Hindu peers, they were less likely to perform formal worship and prayer and more likely to have a more personalised approach. Even more than the other Asian groups they did not doubt that a religious identity would be part of what they would wish to inculcate in their children, for Islam was central to their minority identity.

Despite the importance that the three sets of first generation Asians claimed for religion, there was little support for the idea of religious schools. The only group that could see any value in the idea were the Muslims and even then only two of the eight first generation Muslims said they would send their children to such schools. Everyone else either questioned the quality of academic education that such schools would provide or thought that they would exacerbate communal divisions and racial prejudice. The second generation of each of the three faith communities was of this view and many of them were passionately opposed to such schools. Most of both generations thought that state schools should make better provision to meet the religious needs of minorities and to include their heritage within the curriculum, though some thought that the transmission of religions and languages was the responsibility of families and communities alone. Similarly, the majority of the first generation, including all of the Muslims, were in favour of single-sex secondary schools, especially for girls. A number of second generation women too thought that girls-only schools were academically better for girls.

Marriage partners

A further topic of study was mixed marriages and relationships. In both the Caribbean generations there was some ambivalence about these. Most did not express disapproval and it was generally felt that the choice of partners was down to the individual person. Respondents pointed out, however, the problems that mixed couples would face. Other peoples' attitudes towards mixed relationships and the children were highlighted. Indeed, even the attitude of the white partner was said to be potentially troublesome. Cultural differences were also mentioned as a possible problem. Two respondents argued that mixed relationships should be encouraged as they break down barriers between groups in society. The most emotive issue, however, was a feeling among the second generation of betrayal by those successful black people who had chosen white partners because they thought other black people not good enough for them or likely to be a social handicap.

The marriages of the first generation Asian respondents had been arranged by their parents within their own ethno-religious group. They expected the same for their children, believing this was a sounder basis for a life-long marriage than 'falling in love'. Additionally, Asians voiced several objections to mixed marriages. It was envisaged that the partner in such a marriage would not be interested in or able to fully join the Asian family with its mutual responsibilities. This would weaken family ties and the children would drift away; conversely, in order to succeed in a mixed marriage and a predominantly non-Asian social environment, the Asian partner would lose or suppress his or her culture or religion. Children of such unions would have even fewer roots in Asian family, cultural and religious life. Finally, the first generation respondents pointed to the disapproval in their communities against such marriages, as a result of which a family in which such a marriage took place might suffer a considerable loss of standing. The position of the Muslims was modified by the fact that it was at least theoretically recognised that marriages outside the ethnic group were endorsed by religion as long as the partner was or became a Muslim. The position of the Sikhs and Hindus had undergone some change in that very few respondents mentioned caste as a legitimate consideration.

The second generation Asians took a less clear-cut view, though many of them held diametrically opposed views to those of the first generation. Nearly all of the second generation gave some support to the view that marriage was ultimately a matter of individual choice, and some explicitly argued that colour or ethnic origin was not relevant. On the other hand, most also recognised that the problems mentioned by the first generation were real enough; a few said that romantic love was over-valued and they could not happily marry someone not culturally compatible with their family. Some Indians thought that the problems of drifting away from one's family and culture were not insuperable if sympathetic non-Indian partners were chosen. The majority of the second generation Indians had no objections to mixed marriages and about half of them (though few Muslims) positively approved of cohabiting with a partner as a form of 'trial marriage'. Muslims seemed to entertain least the possibility of marriage to non-Muslims who did not convert to Islam though some thought that conversion was too great a demand to make on one's partner.

The most marked difference between first generation expectations and second generation aspirations, especially among the Indians, was on the custom of parentally arranged marriages. If Asian families have so far avoided serious internal conflict over arranged marriage, this is probably because when it came to the crunch the children accepted their parents' authority, perhaps fearing the consequences of outright conflict, and wanting to avoid the community censure and shame their actions might bring upon the whole family. Parents may be modifying traditional arrangements by incorporating some element of consultation and compromise with the children, but endogamy continues to be the norm, and for the time being marriage remains a principal means of affirming and maintaining an ethnic identity amongst the South Asian groups.

Difference, commonality and exclusion

The predominant term of self-identity amongst the Caribbean respondents was Black, though slightly more common amongst the first generation was West Indian, and amongst the second generation, hyphenated terms like Afro-Caribbean had replaced West Indian and some made reference to British, as in Black British. Black is now firmly established as a term of positive self-identification, colour having replaced specific island-origins, and being allied to a pan-Caribbean identity. For colour is the conspicuous difference noted by the white British and the basis of exclusion. Some second generation respondents thought of themselves as Black British even while appreciating that the white British did not necessarily accept this sharing of an identity. Two respondents, however, felt that a colour-identity was too restrictive and could not encompass the totality of their identity.

Thus, while most had transformed a negative racial description into a positive identity, some worried that even a positive racial identity restricted one's total identity and encouraged the white British to see one as a 'type'. There was little interest in an 'African' identity, unlike in the United States, where 'African-American' is largely replacing 'Black' in public discourse. For some second generation respondents 'Black' referred to all who suffered racism and thus included South Asians. In any case, most thought that, despite the considerable cultural dissimilarities, the experience of racism was a basis of commonality with Asians and some thought that food and family offered other forms of commonality, while others that British youth culture was creating new fusions.

Despite a strong sense of social and cultural commonality with the white British, most Caribbeans found it difficult to lay claim to be British. The difficulty was almost entirely based on the knowledge that the majority of white British people did not acknowledge the commonality and really believed that only white people could be British. The Caribbeans felt that they were constantly reminded that they were not accepted in a variety of ways including discrimination in employment, harassment, invisibility and stereotyping in the media and glorification of an imperial past in which they were oppressed. This racism rather than any sense of distinctive ethnic heritage was seen as an obstacle to feelings of unity with the white British majority.

Most South Asians, especially amongst the first generation, identified with their specific ethnic or religious identity rather than with a pan-Asian ethnicity or British nationality. Religious identification was virtually absent amongst the Punjabi Sikhs who predominantly described themselves as Indians. Pakistanis were alone amongst the first generation in using a hyphenated Pakistani-British description. Such hyphenated descriptions were used by some second generation individuals in each of these groups, and amongst the second generation Punjabis and Gujaratis, 'Asian' was also used. On the whole, the South Asians were as conscious of differences as of similarities between Asians. The Sikhs and Hindus were most likely to refer to each other as the group with whom they had the most in common, and Pakistanis and Bangladeshis pointed to their commonality in Islam. Those who emphasised the differences between Asian groups referred to religion, language, dress and cuisine; those who emphasised the similarities spoke of Asians having religion-centred cultures based on similar family structures and moral codes.

While those for whom Asian was a positive identity were a minority (only half the sample expressed a view), those who rejected the idea were few, and most used the term to describe themselves and their community. A small number of second generation persons, mainly Punjabis, emphasised the importance of a 'black' political identity; for them it highlighted the importance of racism rather than minority cultures in shaping the lives of the non-white minorities, and offered a basis of uniting all these groups in effective anti-racism beyond an emphasis on cultural differences. Most of them, and some other second generation Asians, felt culturally close to young Caribbeans, especially in terms of music, friendships and social life. Most of the second generation respondents and all of the first generation respondents, however, felt there were major dissimilarities between themselves and Caribbeans, instancing religion, language, family structure, marriages, dress and food, and felt that the Caribbeans were much more integrated into British life.

Most Asian respondents thought that being British depended upon more than a legal definition, for example, most first generation Asians thought that their children, schooled and socialised in Britain, were more British than themselves. Equally, they thought that white people did not allow non-whites to be fully British. For themselves, most of the first generation did not claim to be, nor wanted to be, British in this extra-legal sense. They had a strong sense of belonging to the society in which they had been brought up and saw themselves as law-abiding, hard-working citizens at peace with British society but culturally distinct from it. Other first generation respondents, more often male and more educated, saw their citizenship as implying an active interest in British institutions and society, adopting British ways and mixing with all kinds of Britons socially, whilst still maintaining some of their religious and ethnic traditions in a bi-cultural way.

Some of the second generation too saw themselves in terms of a bi-culturalism but the majority felt they were culturally more British than anything else. Few, however, felt they could call themselves British in an unproblematic way. By thinking of Britishness in terms of 'whiteness', backed up by violence, racial discrimination, harassment, abusive jokes and cultural intolerance, some white people made it very difficult for non-whites to identify with Britain in a positive way. Those who saw themselves in terms of a bi-cultural or hyphenated identity were, however, usually positive about being British and did not think that there was an inevitable conflict between the two sides of their identity. A minority of second generation Asians, however, felt alienated from British culture which they perceived as hostile to their family-centred and religious values.

Ethnic identity and the future

This study, then, shows how ethnic identity, far from being some primordial stamp upon an individual, is a plastic and changing badge of membership. Ethnic identity is a product of a number of forces: social exclusion and stigma and political resistance to them, distinctive cultural and religious heritages as well as new forms of culture, communal and familial loyalties, marriage practices, coalition of interests and so on. Hence, the boundaries of groups are unclear and shifting, especially when groups seek to broaden an ethnic identity or to accommodate membership in a number of overlapping groups. And this leaves out the broader social, economic and political forces.

What is clear is that, while considerable cultural adaptation has taken place and is still taking place, the predictions of an unproblematic assimilationist 'melting pot' have proven to be sociologically naive

(Parekh, 1990). Minority ethnicity is neither simply a racist attribution nor a set of private practices but, symbolically and materially, has become a feature of British society with all that implies for public identities, political solidarities and competition for resources. It also means a rethinking of Britishness and the varieties and forms that it can encompass.

Our research shows, we believe, that the emerging and evolving plurality on the ground, especially when allied to developments in mixed ethnicity relationships which we have not explored, belies those who argue that the infusion of new cultural groups is disruptive to social cohesion and British identity. It challenges those who think in terms of the simplistic oppositions of British-Alien or Black-White. A significant population on the ground is living in ways that refute these dualisms. It is time for social analysts and policy-makers to catch up. We need a new vision of Britishness which allows minorities to make a claim upon it, to be accepted as British regardless of their colour and origins, and without having to conform to a narrow cultural norm.

References

Ali, Y. (1991) 'Echoes of Empire: Towards A Politics of Representation', in Cromer, J. and Harvey, S. (eds), *Enterprise and Heritage: Cross Currents of National Culture,* Routledge, pp.194-211.

Alleyne, M. (1988) *Roots of Jamaican Culture,* Pluto Press.

Anthias, F. and Yuval-Davis, N. (1992) *Racialised Boundaries: Race, Nation, Gender, Colour and Class and The Anti-Racist Struggle,* Routledge.

Anwar, M. (1993) *Muslims in Britain: 1991 Census and Other Statistical Sources,* Centre for the Study of Islam and Christian-Muslim Relations Papers, Birmingham.

Back, L. (1993) 'Race, Identity and Nation Within An Adolescent Community in South London', *New Community,* 19(2):217-233.

Baldwin-Edwards, M. and Schain, M.A. (eds) (1994) 'The Politics of Immigration in Western Europe', Special Issue, *West European Politics,* 17(2) April.

Ballard, R. and Kalra, V.S. (1994) *The Ethnic Dimensions of the 1991 Census: A Preliminary Report,* Manchester Census Group, University of Manchester.

Banton, M. (1979) 'It's Our Country', in Miles, R. and Phizaclea, A. (eds) *Racism and Political Action in Britain,* Routledge, pp.233-246.

Barth, F. (1969) *Ethnic Groups and Boundaries,* Allen and Unwin.

Baumann, G. (1994) *The Politics of Identity: Two Discourses of 'Culture' and 'Community' in a Suburb of London,* Monograph in preparation.

Berry, J.W. et al (1987) 'Comparative Studies of Acculturative Stress', *International Migration Review,* 21:491-511.

Bonnett, A. (1993) *Radicalism, Anti-Racism and Representation,* Routledge.

Boulton, M.J and Smith, P. (1992) 'Ethnic Preferences and Perceptions Among Asian and White British Middle School Children', *Social Development,* 1(1):55-66.

Brooks, D. (1975) *Race and Labour in London Transport,* Oxford University Press.

Burgess, R.G. (1984) *In The Field: An Introduction to Field Research,* Allen and Unwin.

Byron, M. (1992) 'The Caribbean-Britain Migration Cycle: Migrant Goals, Social Networks and Socio-Economic Structure', D.Phil Thesis, University of Oxford.

Centre for Contemporary Cultural Studies (CCCS) (1982) *The Empire Strikes Back,* Hutchinson.

Cohen, P. (1988) 'The Perversions of Inheritance: Studies in the Making of Multi-Racist Britain', in Cohen, P. and Bains, H.S. (eds) *Multi-Racist Britain,* Macmillan.

Commission for Racial Equality (CRE) (1988) 'Ethnic Classification System Recommended by CRE', Press Statement, 7 December.

Commission for Racial Equality (CRE) (1990) *Britain: A Plural Society,* CRE.

Daniel, W.W. (1968) *Racial Discrimination in England,* Penguin.

Dench, G. (1993) *From Extended Family to State Dependency,* Centre for Community Studies, Middlesex University.

Dennis, F. (1989) 'The Black Family in Crisis', *The Standard,* 23 August.

Donald, J. and Rattansi, A. (eds) (1992) *'Race', Culture and Difference,* Sage.

Drew, D., Gray, J. and Sime, N. (1992) *Against The Odds: The Education and Labour Market Experiences of Black Young People,* Research and Development No. 68 – Youth Cohort Series No. 19, Department of Employment.

Drury, B. (1991) 'Sikh Girls and the Maintenance of an Ethnic Culture', *New Community,* 17(3):387-399.

Drury, B. (1992) 'The Impact of Religion, Culture, Racism and Politics on The Multiple Identities of Sikh Girls', Conference on Culture, Identity and Politics: Ethnic Minorities in Britain, 9 May, St. Anthoy's College, Oxford.

Francome, C. (1994) *The Great Leap: A Study of 107 Hindu and Sikh Students,* Middlesex University.

Fuchs, L.H. (1990) *The American Kaleidoscope: Race, Ethnicity and the Civic Culture,* University Press of New England: Hanover and London.

Ghuman, P.A.S. (1994) *Coping With Two Cultures: British Asian and Indo-Canadian Adolescents,* Multilingual Matters, Clevedon.

Gillborn, D. (1991) *'Race', Ethnicity and Education,* Routledge.

Gillborn, D. (1995) *Racism and Anti-Racism in Real Schools,* Open University Press.

Gillroy, P. (1987) *There Ain't No Black in the Union Jack,* Hutchinson.

Goldberg, D.T. (1993) *Racist Culture,* Blackwell.

Hall, S. (1992) 'New Ethnicities', in Donald and Rattansi (eds) (1992) pp. 252-259.

Hammersley, M. and Atkinson, P. (1983) *Ethnography: Principles in Practice,* Tavistock.

Haynes, A. (1983) *The State of Black Britain,* Root Books.

Heath, S. and Dale, A. (1994) 'Household and Family Formation in Great Britain: The Ethnic Dimension', *Population Studies,* 7:5-13.

House of Commons Home Affairs Committee (1982-83 session), *Ethnic and Racial Question in the Census, vol. 2: Minutes of Evidence,* HMSO.

Hutnik, N. (1991) *Ethnic Minority Identity, A Social Psychological Perspective,* Clarendon Press, Oxford.

James, W. (1993) 'Migration, Racism and Identity Formations: The Caribbean Experience in Britain', in James, W. and Harris, C. (eds) *Inside Babylon: The Caribbean Diaspora in Britain,* Verso.

Jayaweera, H. (1993) 'Racial Disadvantage and Ethnic Identity: The Experiences of Afro-Caribbean Women in a British City', *New Community,* 19(3):383-406.

Jones, T. (1993) *Britain's Ethnic Minorities,* Policy Studies Institute.

Keith, M. (1993) *Race, Riots and Policing: Lore and Disorder in a Multi-Racist Society,* UCL Press.

Knott, K. and Khokher, S. (1993) 'Religious and Ethnic Identity Among Young Muslim Women in Bradford', *New Community,* 19(4): 593-610.

Lal, B.B. (1990) *The Romance of Culture in an Urban Civilisation,* Routledge.

Mac An Ghaill, M. (1988) *Young, Gifted and Black,* Open University Press.

Mendus, S. (1989) *Toleration and the Limits of Liberalism,* Macmillan.

Midgett, D. (1975) 'West Indian Ethnicity in Great Britain', in Safa, H. and du Toit, B. (eds) *Migration and Development,* Mouton.

Modood, T. (1988) '"Black", Racial Equality and Asian Identity', *New Community,* 14(3):397-404.

Modood, T. (1990) 'British Asian Muslims and the Rushdie Affair', *Political Quarterly,* 61(2):143-160; reproduced in Donald and Rattansi (1992): 260-267.

Modood, T. (1992) *Not Easy Being British: Colour, Culture and Citizenship,* Runnymede Trust and Trentham Books.

Modood, T. (1994a) *Racial Equality: Colour, Culture and Justice,* Commission on Social Justice, Issue Paper No. 5, Institute of Public Policy Research.

Modood, T. (1994b) 'Political Blackness and British Asians', *Sociology,* 28(3).

Modood, T. (1994c) 'Muslim Identity: Social Reality or Political Project?', in *Muslim Identity: Real or Imagined?* A discussion by John Rex and Tariq Modood, CSIC Paper Europe No.12, Selly Oak Colleges, Birmingham.

Modood, T. (1995) 'The Limits of America: Rethinking Equality in the Changing Context of British Race Relations', in Ward, B. and Badger, T. (eds) *The Making of Martin Luther King and the Civil Rights Movement,* Macmillan.

Modood, T. and Shiner, M. (1994) *Ethnic Minorities and Higher Education: Why Are There Differential Rates of Entry?,* Policy Studies Institute.

Ouseley, H. (1993) 'Young, Single and Black', *The Independent,* 2 July.

Parekh, B. (1990) 'Britain and the Social Logic of Pluralism', in Commission for Racial Equality (1990).

Parsons, G. (1993) 'Filling a Void? Afro-Caribbean Identity and Religion', in Parsons, G. (ed) *The Growth of Religious Diversity: Britain From 1945; Volume 1: Traditions,* Routledge and Open University.

Pollard, P. (1972) 'Jamaicans and Trinidadians in North London', *New Community,* 1(5):370-377.

Robinson, V. (1991) 'Goodbye Yellow Brick Road: The Spatial Mobility and Immobility of Britain's Ethnic Population 1971-81', *New Community,* 17(3): 313-330.

Senior, O. (1991) *Working Miracles: Women's Lives in the English-Speaking Caribbean,* James Currey.

Shaw, A. (1988) *A Pakistani Community in Britain,* Blackwell.

Smith, A. (1981) *The Ethnic Revival in the Modern World,* Cambridge University Press.

Smith, A.M. (1994) 'Rastafari as Resistance and the Ambiguities of Essentialism in the "New Social Movements"', in Laclau, E. (ed) *The Making of Political Identities,* Verso.

Smith, D.J. (1977) *Racial Disadvantage in Britain,* Penguin Books.

Smith, D.J. and Tomlinson, S. (1989) *The School Effect: A Study of Multi-Racial Comprehensives,* Policy Studies Institute.

Stopes-Roe, M. and Cochrane, R. (1990) *Citizens of This Country: The Asian-British,* Multilingual Matters.

Tizard, B. and Phoenix, A. (1993) *Black, White or Mixed Race?,* Routledge.

Troyna, B. (1993) *Racism and Education: Research Perspectives,* Open University Press.

Vertovec, S. (1993) *Local Contexts and the Development of Muslim Communities in Britain: Observations in Keighley, West Yorkshire,* unpublished.

Virdee, S. (1995) *Racial Violence and Harassment,* Policy Studies Institute.

Watson, J.L. (ed) (1977) *Between Two Cultures: Migrants and Minorities in Britain.*

Young, I.M. (1990) *Justice and the Politics of Difference,* Princeton University Press.

Young, M. and Willmott, P. (1957) *Family and Kinship in East London,* Routledge.